STRENGTHENING YOUR STEPFAMILY

Elizabeth Einstein
& Linda Albert

AGS®
American Guidance Service
Circle Pines, Minnesota 55014-1796

AGS staff participating in the development and production of this publication:

Program Division
Dorothy Chapman, Director
Bonnie Goldsmith, Senior Project Editor
Janice Cauley, Copy Editor

Support Services
David Youngquist, Director
Lynne Cromwell, Production Coordinator
Carol McLean, Production Manager
Maureen Wilson, Art Director
Sylvia Carsen, Production Artist

Project Editor
Marjorie Lisovskis

Art Editor
Diane LeTendre

Design
Terry Dugan, Terry Dugan Design

Illustrations
John Bush

Library of Congress Catalog Card Number: 85-73867
ISBN 0-88671-217-3
A   10   9   8   7   6   5   4

To my mother, Betty Mae Higbie, whose wise choice of a remarriage partner gave me the gift of a wonderful and loving stepfather.
E. E.

Love and gratitude to my son, Ken Moraff, who survived and thrived in a stepfamily before I knew the information presented in the pages that follow.
L. A.

Other Works by the Authors

Elizabeth Einstein ——————————————————————

The Stepfamily: Living, Loving, and Learning
Stepfamily Living Series (with Linda Albert)

Linda Albert ——————————————————————————

Coping with Kids
Coping with Kids and School
Coping with Kids and Vacations
Stepfamily Living Series (with Elizabeth Einstein)

CONTENTS

Introduction

Both John and Amy had custody of their children when they met and began dating. John's wife had died nine months before, about the same time Amy separated from her husband. Both were doing the best they could to take care of their children, but to spend a lot of time alone together they often shared a sitter. John wined and dined Amy and she found their courtship exciting. Though her former husband called frequently, she put him off, preferring to be with her new love. Once Amy's divorce was final, she and John married. After a brief honeymoon, they returned to live in John's house with her three children and his two.

Amy and John dreamed they could make marriage better the second time around. But as they settled into the first few weeks of stepfamily living, the couple found themselves repeating the patterns of their previous lifestyles. Things became difficult when Amy's former husband called to discuss unresolved issues about the children. Sometimes their telephone conversations ended in arguments. John often felt resentful and jealous when Amy spent a lot of time talking with her ex-husband. But he didn't tell Amy how he felt; nor did she tell him how guilty she had begun to feel for not loving his children the way she did her own. Privately, neither believed their relationship could hold up if such feelings were brought into the open. Amy's children wanted to spend more time alone with her, but they kept quiet for fear they would anger their new stepfather. They worried that he, too, might leave. No one talked about any of these feelings and little trust developed among family members.

Within months, child-rearing problems intensified. Amy believed in strict rules and severe punishment; John felt that if the children were allowed to make their own decisions, they would do fine. He threatened them when they misbehaved but rarely followed through. His parenting style was indeed a contrast to Amy's. They tried his way, then her way. But they never developed an "our" way—a discipline approach they both felt comfortable with.

Soon the chaos became too much. John and Amy agreed to see a counselor, but they could neither clarify nor resolve their differences. Within two years they divorced.

As Susan and Paul left their parenting class, they agreed that this investment in strengthening their stepfamily was one of the best they could have made. Early in their marriage, they realized they each had a very different approach to discipline. After much confusion, they decided to go together and learn some child-rearing skills. There were too many good things about their family life to let this problem create a conflict.

Things felt right for Paul and Susan. After divorcing, both had taken time to redefine relationships with their former spouses. Susan's first husband had moved to the West Coast. Her children only saw their father on long visits twice a year, but he regularly kept in touch with them through postcards, tapes, short notes, and a weekly telephone call. Paul's former wife had remained in the local community. She and Paul shared custody of their children, who spent alternate weeks in each home. Susan and Paul understood the importance of the children's continued contact with their other parents and supported shared parenthood however they could.

As single parents, Paul and Susan had both dated a variety of people and consequently felt they knew what they wanted in a relationship. Paul had attended workshops for divorced and single adults and had read several books that helped him recognize and understand how he had behaved in his former marriage and how he now felt. Susan had returned to college and earned her degree in management—a long-cherished dream. She liked the full-time job she had since taken on. During their courtship, Susan and Paul had discussed having more children. Paul was already supporting four and money loomed as a future problem area. Still, Susan looked forward to the day when she and Paul would have their own child. After seeing they could both manage careers and expenses with enough income left over to pay for child care and household help, he agreed that adding an "ours" child to their lives would be possible.

At first, the couple considered moving into Susan's roomy old house, which could easily accommodate their large stepfamily, but they decided it would be wiser to make a fresh start. They found a house that was new to everyone and let the children help make decisions about their rooms.

The first year of marriage was challenging. Paul and Susan had very different ways of doing things and they argued about who was right. Paul missed daily contact with his children; he sometimes felt guilty. Susan struggled to keep up with her job and find enough time for Paul and her children. Realizing she felt indifferent toward Paul's children, Susan worried that something was wrong with her. She began to think it might be better not to have a child of their own. Although Susan and Paul were able to talk with each other about their feelings, they couldn't resolve them, and their concerns deepened. After months of continual arguments about discipline, the couple finally agreed to talk with a professional counselor.

The counselor listened as Paul and Susan shared their concerns. Both feared that their new family was failing and that pressure was creating more stress. Although they believed some confusion was normal, they didn't believe their problems would just go away. Susan and Paul spent two sessions with the counselor, clarifying some expectations. They also learned about a local support group for stepfamilies. After attending a few meetings, they began to realize that their problems were not all that different from other stepparents'. Their fears lessened. They began to spend more time together and, as their relationship strengthened, many of the problems diminished. They began to have faith in their love for each other and the process of making a stepfamily. When they still couldn't agree on discipline, someone in the support group told them about a parenting class at the local school.

Paul and Susan had been told that stepfamily living held many challenges; now they knew how true this was! But they also knew their commitment to meeting those challenges would make the difference.

Two stepfamily scenarios. Two different ways of approaching the challenge of remarriage with children. And two very different results.

By taking remarriage preparation too lightly and believing some myths about stepfamily living, Amy and John had developed unrealistic expectations for their new life together. When these hopes and dreams remained unfulfilled, they both began to feel disappointed and defeated. In addition to naive expectations, neither John nor Amy had good parenting skills, and each had different ideas about raising children. The resulting discipline dilemma caused trouble for their new stepfamily. Amy's children began to feel angry at their mother, resentful toward their stepfather. The behavior of all the children worsened. Through all of this, everyone kept quiet and avoided discussing feelings. Soon, everything got out of control. Too soon remarried, with too little helpful information and inadequate skills, Amy and John denied their ever-increasing family problems and soon became another remarriage divorce statistic.

Paul and Susan did it differently. Before forming a stepfamily, they took time to complete important personal growth tasks. Each worked on improving relations with the former spouse. During their courtship, they dealt with the specifics of where to live, how to earn money, whether to have another child. After their remarriage, they shared their fears and feelings; when they had difficulties, they sought support.

Nodding or shaking your head as you recall the stages of making a stepfamily, you may identify with John and Amy or Susan and Paul. Maybe you began your own stepfamily following one pattern or the other. Like John and Amy, you might have built your stepfamily on unrealistic hopes and expectations. Or, like Susan and Paul, you might have tried to learn something about the stepfamily—by reading a book, attending a lecture, or talking with others who live in stepfamilies. Perhaps your approach was, or is, somewhere in between.

Stepfamilies *can* work well. Many people who live in this special kind of family reap rich rewards. Through a commitment to make your stepfamily successful, coupled with skills and information you can learn and apply over time, you too can find pride and satisfaction.

Some cynics say the idea of "family" is dying; reality shows otherwise. While families used to exist to fill an economic need, the modern family's focus is on fulfilling emotional needs. A happy family life—in whatever form—still remains the goal of most people.

Many kinds of families exist today. Most likely you've already lived in several. You were born into your biological family, often called your *family of origin.* Years later, you may have married and created a nuclear family, which may have produced children. If that family ended, through divorce or the death of your mate, you may have become part of a single-parent family, either rearing your children alone or sharing parenthood with your former spouse. Now, upon remarriage, you will have started a stepfamily. Each is a real family in which children can be reared successfully and a sense of love, unity, and happiness can be achieved.

A healthy stepfamily may be large or relatively small. Different custody and shared parenthood arrangements produce full-time or part-time stepfamilies. Sometimes adults with children live together but are not legally married; they too comprise a kind of stepfamily. For our definition purposes, a stepfamily is a family in which at least one of the adult partners has children from a prior relationship.

Many people wonder how the stepfamily got its name. The term is rooted in the Anglo-Saxon word *steopchild,* meaning bereaved or orphaned child. Cinderella was one such child, and stories like hers have helped give the word *stepfamily* a generally negative image. At one time, most stepfamilies formed after the death of a parent. Today most begin following a divorce and single-parent family living. Some people have tried to create a new name for the stepfamily. Adjectives like *blended, recoupled, remarried, binuclear, combined, prefabricated, reconstituted,* and even *synergistic* have all been used to describe this special family form. New labels, however, are merely new masks. They cover up an important reality: the stepfamily is a different kind of family with special obstacles and opportunities, special strengths and stresses. Changing the name of your family helps little; learning how it works is what will make a difference.

Whether you are considering remarriage, are living together, or have lived in a stepfamily for some time, you can learn to build a healthy family life, making your stepfamily strengths work for you. To make your stepfamily successful, to build from your differences rather than deny them, you need to understand the inherent challenges you face. By focusing on specific relationships within the stepfamily, *Strengthening Your Stepfamily* will help you come to understand both the problems and the potential of your stepfamily.

Chapter 1 focuses on helping you learn about your stepfamily structure, how it differs from your previous family structure. You'll examine common myths and unrealistic expectations that can invite trouble. This chapter also discusses ways families can begin coping with guilt and loss in order to start building better, stronger stepfamily relations.

Chapter 2 focuses on your couple relationship—the key to stepfamily stability. You will identify strengths and weaknesses in your relationship and learn the importance of communicating and sharing feelings. This exploration may point up some important premarital tasks that have been left undone; the chapter will guide you to back up and work on them so your family can move forward.

Chapter 3 explores the basic ingredients for building positive relations between stepparents and stepchildren. As newcomers and additions to what was recently a single-parent family, stepparents are often confused about their role. How should they act and interact with their new stepchildren? Although they need to develop effective relationships, stepparents find no existing models or rules to follow. Focusing on adult-child dynamics in the stepfamily, this chapter explores the many ways adults and children can relate and suggests guidelines for doing so.

Chapter 4 addresses children in the stepfamily. It examines their loyalty conflicts, their sense of loss, the lack of control they feel. As you consider these factors, you will be given suggestions and guidelines for helping children adjust to stepparents, stepsiblings, stepgrandparents, multiple households, and new family structures.

Chapter 5 describes the developmental process of making a stepfamily, stressing the importance of allowing enough time. The focus is on the entire family unit and the merging of two separate ways of doing things. As you explore issues ranging from daily routines to holiday traditions and celebrations, you will sense a family history beginning to take shape.

There are many special, rich rewards for you to anticipate from stepfamily living. Challenges that, at first, seem troublesome or even overwhelming can lead to growth and expanded horizons for all family members. Through *Strengthening Your Stepfamily* you will gain information and skills that can lead your family to success. Your commitment is the only other tool required.

Understanding the Pitfalls and Potential of Stepfamily Living

I t took me a long time to realize that divorce didn't **end** my family—it simply changed it. Now, remarriage has changed it again. Trudy and the kids haven't replaced anybody or anything in my life: better than that, they've **added** to it. Our stepfamily is a very special kind of family!"

The stepfamily *is* a special kind of family. The variety of backgrounds, past experiences, and values that go into making it offer the potential for a family life that is as enriching as it is challenging. Meeting the challenge of stepfamily living requires patience and perseverance, knowledge and skills. The more awareness you gain early on, the smoother and steadier your progress will be. This journey to success is a process; it takes time. Depending on the amount of preparation done by both partners before such a marriage, it can take up to several years for a stepfamily to stabilize—for everyone to be comfortable with one another. While this may seem like a long time, just recall how much you and your children have been through until now. If you have not married or been a parent before and are now a stepparent, it's important that you understand all the changes your mate and his or her children have experienced, so your expectations will be realistic.

The information in this chapter provides a foundation your stepfamily can build on. Your family, like others, will be affected by stress; but, understanding what is happening, you will be better able to cope. First, your entire family needs to recognize a basic reality: the stepfamily is a special kind of family. Much of the material in this chapter will explore why this is so. Next, the chapter will examine myths and misinformation that can create unrealistic expectations and lead to trouble. The last part of the chapter discusses ways you can begin to resolve feelings of guilt and loss in order to start building better, stronger, stepfamily relationships.

Stepfamilies Are Different

"We are a special kind of family." When you and your family members can make this positive statement about living in a stepfamily, you will be on your way to reaching your potential. A stepfamily is not worse than, better than, or a substitute for other families in which you have lived: it is simply different.

Too often, stepfamilies deny this fact. Consciously or unconsciously, they try to be like the families they just came from—only better. This causes unnecessary stress and leads many stepfamilies down the path to trouble. But understanding and accepting that the stepfamily is different provides a strong foundation for success. It allows family members to build on those special qualities that make their stepfamily one of a kind.

Born of Loss

A newly formed stepfamily is often a paradox: hand in hand with joy and hope lingers sadness. You may feel depressed and your children seem sad—just when you'd hoped everyone would be happy. If the future looks so rosy, why are you feeling blue? As changes take place, everyone in your stepfamily is confronting loss in some specific way. Two people entering marriage for the first time usually haven't experienced the major losses of death or divorce that all members of a new stepfamily have known. These losses affect the very character of the stepfamily. As they are identified, mourned, and let go, the stepfamily can move to a higher level of awareness and satisfaction.

Kids have lost control, contact, and continuity. No one in the stepfamily has experienced more loss than the children. They had no choice in parental decisions, yet their lives have been changed forever. Most likely, children have lost daily contact with one parent. They may have had to move. If so, they lost major touchstones: school, teachers, home, perhaps their own room. They also lost contact with schoolmates, neighborhood friends, and familiar activities. Financial changes may have created many losses as well. If, for example, their mother began working outside the home, or changed from a part-time to a full-time job, the children probably lost some of the attention they were accustomed to when she was more available to them.

As time passed and everyone pulled together to make things work, the kids probably adjusted to life in a single-parent family. Many children recall that they liked the special family closeness and personal attention they experienced during that time. But remarriage threatens this closeness; it represents yet another in the series of changes your family has undergone. The hardest thing children of remarriage must learn is to share a parent—not only with stepsiblings, but with another adult. Many children harbor the fantasy that one day their parents will work things out and get back together—that their family will be restored. Remarriage may force these children to confront their loss. Depending upon their age and psychological maturity, children may respond to remarriage much as they did to divorce or parental death. Chapter 4, "The Stepchild's Dilemmas," explores these losses further.

The biological parent has lost status and stability. Between marriages you experienced many losses, some of which you may not have recognized. They began with the loss of a marriage partner—and of the structure, status, and stability that marriage provided. When the marriage relationship ended, your self-esteem might have slipped—your courage might have disappeared as you faced the future alone in a strange new role. You might have blamed yourself for the divorce, wondering, "What's the matter with me?" And, like many divorced people, you might also have suffered a great financial loss, forcing you to make radical changes in the way you live. It is important that you become aware of these losses and acknowledge them.

One of the most difficult things divorced parents face is the loss of daily contact with their children. In the past, it was usually men who coped with this; today, as fathers take a greater role in their children's lives, women are facing such a loss as well. Absentee mothers say they never dreamed it would be so painful. The stigma attached to noncustodial parents—mothers especially—and the lack of support they receive from society serve to compound their loss.

Upon remarriage, the parent whose children live elsewhere often takes on the responsibility of the new spouse's children. For many, daily interaction with stepchildren intensifies the pain of losing contact with their own children. Parents cut off from their biological children often feel guilty: to compensate, they may respond by avoiding a serious commitment to stepchildren. This holding back (often unconscious) does little to build respect and trust within the stepfamily. Yet stepchildren have already lost much of their faith in adults and themselves, and so building trust is essential.

For some new stepparents, a long-held marriage dream is shattered. People not previously married who choose divorced or widowed partners may become stepparents before ever having been biological parents. They too face a loss: the loss of privacy and intimacy they had imagined would be part of their newlywed bliss. Fresh from the ceremony, these stepparents face the "instant family" they've acquired—perhaps far different from their dream family. Visions of romantic dinners and cozy times alone with their new spouse become realities of hot dogs and miniature-golf games with the kids. And, when a dream is shattered, that part of a person's self invested in the dream also seems lost and is soon replaced with resentment and hostility.

Later in this chapter we'll look at ways to begin dealing with the losses that are part of a stepfamily's makeup.

Nonresidential Parent

One of the most important differences between the stepfamily and the traditional nuclear family is the "presence" of the nonresidential parent. That parent may be physically absent from the daily scene in the stepfamily home, but he or she is psychologically present to everyone living there. As a custodial parent or a stepparent, you might wish you could change this fact. But

A different kind of family creates a different kind of honeymoon.

although the role your child's other parent once played in *your* life has changed, one reality will never change: that person will always be your child's parent. Depending upon how old your children were when your marriage ended, they had probably already developed an identity and sense of well-being that came, in part, from the other parent. Whatever contact and closeness this parent can continue to provide will be essential to your child's psychological well-being.

Children reap the rewards when you transform your relationship to their other parent from mate to coparent. Ultimately, so do you. When you and your former spouse can respect one another, each of you will feel good about yourself and be a better parent.

To a great extent, your children's ability to continue the relationship with their other parent is up to you. Under the strain of the separation and divorce, you may have said some harsh things about this person, fostering a negative image of the parent in your children's eyes. If your relationship with your former spouse *remains* a negative one, continued unresolved feelings may be played out through the children. This will hurt them and damage your relationship with them. When your relationship with their other parent is neutral or positive, the children can be free of loyalty conflicts. They can grow up knowing they are valued and loved by both parents. Children reap the rewards when you transform your relationship to this person from mate to coparent. Ultimately, so do you. When you and your former spouse can respect one another, each of you will feel good about yourself and be a better parent. Further, the more positive your attitude toward your former mate, the greater the chance that your children will adjust to their new stepparent. They will feel no need to defend their missing parent.

If you are a stepparent, your acceptance of the other biological parent as a stepfamily reality is a loving gift to your spouse and stepchildren. You can be an addition to, not a replacement in, their lives.

Children Move Between Two Homes

Regardless of legal custody arrangements, your children will most likely move between Mom's place and Dad's. Whether they spend every weekend or a single month each summer in the other home, children need to feel that they belong, can learn life's lessons, and are expected to contribute and be responsible in both families.

At best, moving between two homes is not easy: transitions never are. Parting from loved family members is difficult for children *and* adults. Children have to cope with friends and possessions being in two places. They face two sets of rules and routines. Too many children are treated as visitors or guests in the nonresidential parent's home, sleeping on sofas and living out of suitcases. When this happens, children are likely to feel that they don't belong, that they are intruders rather than family members.

Helping children thrive while they travel between homes begins with helping them develop a sense of belonging—of being supported and wanted by others. To do this, parents can provide a permanent space for each child—a room, corner, cupboard, or drawer—depending on the space available. They can display children's artwork year-round, whether the children are there or not. They can include the children in family plans, made by letter or telephone if a child can't be present to be consulted. Belonging, learning, contributing: this trio fosters psychological and emotional well-being.

In spite of the difficulties, many long-term benefits can result. Children who move between two homes are offered new learning opportunities. The physical reality of living with two families in two places broadens children's horizons. It allows them to see different lifestyles and family systems. Stepchildren may gain travel experience; and two geographies provide new friends, different customs and activities.

If you are a stepparent, your acceptance of the other biological parent as a stepfamily reality is a loving gift to your spouse and stepchildren. You can be an addition to, not a replacement in, their lives.

Psychological strength can be another benefit. As children develop relationships with two families, they learn to view life from different perspectives. Parents and stepparents may offer new skills, values, or ways to cope. Stepsiblings may introduce new and different interests and hobbies. When faced with decisions, children exposed to these varied approaches will have two sets of experience to draw from.

Stepfamily couples, too, can benefit from children's coming and going. The nonresidential couple can find a child's time in their home enjoyable and enriching. For many, it can open new vistas in their marriage: if young people aren't part of the usual daily scene, interacting with visiting children might bring a refreshing new dimension to the couple's relationship. For the couple in a custodial home, the time the children spend with their other family gives the adults special time together to work on their relationship—or to play together!

Previous Parent-Child Relationships

Because the children existed before the stepfamily did, previous relationships and understandings did too. This is another important stepfamily difference.

As a biological parent, you have shared many years of memories and alliances with your children. When conflict arises, it is natural to align yourself with your children—after all, you are really defending your own identity and child-rearing methods. Stepparents need to accept this tendency and try to avoid feeling rejected or unfairly treated.

The relationship between biological parents and their children is a long-standing one. Further, the longer they have lived in a single-parent family before the remarriage, the stronger the child-parent bond has grown. A stepparent's relationship with such a parent and child may, on the other hand, be relatively recent. When stepparents come to understand this strong existing bond—biological, legal, and emotional—they can focus on building friendship with their stepchildren. As rules and roles are explored, this friendship will allow stepfamily members to function in a relatively neutral family territory, reducing the pressure some members might feel to love each other overnight. The chapters that follow provide guidelines for building these new stepfamily relationships.

Different Family Backgrounds

In most families, people share a common background. Rituals and routines are understood; unspoken rules are often quite clear. Everyone knows how and where holidays and traditions will be celebrated. Religious practices are generally shared by all family members.

Since stepfamily members share no common history, traditions may at first collide.

In stepfamilies, however, people come together with diverse histories and expectations. At first, these different backgrounds may create confusion; later, as family members learn more about each other's histories, negotiate new traditions, and make new memories together, the differences can enrich family life. As they learn alternative ways of thinking and behaving, people in stepfamilies gain a broader view of life and teach each other helpful living skills. Acceptance helps merge two families into one.

Stepfamily traditions can be built around sharing so many things! Here are just a few possibilities:

- The stepfamily's anniversary
- Friday-night suppers

- The first day of spring
- The first snowfall of the year
- A monthly spaghetti night
- A stepfamily journal or scrapbook
- Sunday-night charades
- Any number of other dates, events, or activities meaningful to the stepfamily

Lack of Legal Relationships

In traditional families, everyone is legally related. These legal ties provide family members with rights to insurance, inheritance, medical attention, access to school records, and other important benefits; above all, this legal relationship represents a commitment between adults and children. In the stepfamily, a legal bond exists between the husband and wife but not between stepparents and stepchildren. In most states and provinces the law does not recognize this adult-child relationship. Stepfamily issues such as custody, visitation, and child support may be decided by the court, but the court's decisions are subject to individual circumstances, state or local statutes, and different interpretations.

If a remarriage ends, stepparents have no legal right to a continued relationship with children to whom they may have developed strong personal ties. While stepparents have, in some instances, been granted visitation rights or custody, a ruling of this sort is still unusual. Each case is determined by such factors as the length of the relationship, the motive for seeking visitation or custody, the role the stepparent plays in the child's life, and the quality of that child's relationship with the biological parent.

The law, with regard to the stepfamily, remains filled with inconsistencies. Family mediation, child custody and support, visitation rights, inheritance, insurance, tuition, medical expenses, and adoption are all areas that need to be addressed in an effort to clarify and improve the legal aspects of stepfamily living. It will take expanded social awareness to instigate the necessary legislative and judicial changes. Adults in stepfamilies need to advocate for thorough examination of current laws and practices before changes will come about.

Clearing the Way

There are many obstacles in the stepfamily's search for satisfaction and success. Unrealistic, undisclosed, and unexamined expectations are one. Unexplored myths are another. Both these troublemakers are caused by a lack of information.

Examining Expectations

Unrealistic expectations are stumbling blocks for any family. For the stepfamily such expectations, positive or negative, can cause extra pressure or become self-fulfilling prophecies.

Many adults hope to make up to their children for past hurts. In remarriage, they anticipate another chance to succeed. Their expectations are positive and they view their situation in terms of gains. Children, older ones especially, who sometimes tend to take a more negative view of their parent's remarriage, may feel anxious. With fairy tales providing a poor stepfamily image, some children may actually feel dread and apprehension, fearing the worst. If they have lived in a single-parent family for a long time, or sense that contact with their other biological parent will be diminished, they may view the remarriage in terms of losses.

All of us carry hidden agendas—unspoken plans or wishes for what we want to have happen. Communicating brings expectations—adults' and children's—out into the open. It is essential for a couple to talk about their hopes and needs, and helpful for the children to do so also. If you are forming a new stepfamily, or living in a stepfamily in which you suspect expectations may be vastly different, unclear, or unmet, now is the time for you and your spouse to start clarifying these issues:

Roles. How will each of you relate to your stepchildren? What are your rights and obligations where they're concerned? Who will discipline whom?

Rules and responsibilities. Who will take care of which household chores? How are rules to be enforced? Who'll feed the dog? Take the children to the dentist?

Your relationship with your spouse. When will you spend time alone together? How often will you go away without the children? How will you communicate your fears? Resolve differences? Grow together?

Your relationship with the nonresidential parent. What issues with the nonresidential parent(s) still need to be resolved? What level of involvement do you expect from the other parent? Can you coparent with this former mate without causing your spouse to feel threatened?

Possible custody changes. Can you handle having your spouse's children come to live with you? How would you feel if your child should ask to live with your former spouse? What will you do if this happens?

Work and money. Will both of you work outside the home? How will the two of you manage child-care duties? Who'll pay for what? Will you be a "one-pot" family or keep separate accounts?

Love and remarriage. Have both of you mourned the losses of former marriages? Let go of failure feelings about divorce? What do you expect from your couple relationship?

Children and stepchildren. Do you have certain expectations about how two sets of children should get along? How children are to relate to the adults? How do you plan to help the process work smoothly? What pressures are you feeling about accepting or loving each other's children? What pressures are the children feeling in this marriage? Have children completed mourning earlier losses?

If you don't discuss these issues, how can either of you possibly know what is expected or whether it's possible to meet those expectations? Can you identify other areas of stepfamily living where you may have unclarified expectations?

"Should we move to a new home?"

"Should we have a baby?"

Here and in other chapters we'll examine many of these issues and explore ways to address them.

Debunking the Myths

Myths are based on misperceptions and stereotypes. They are fiction—fabrication, figments of people's imagination. Myths are closely linked to expectations and can create misery in the stepfamily: when life isn't what stepfamily members expected, they may feel disappointed, inadequate, even profoundly discouraged. Some common stepfamily myths are far removed from reality:

Myth: **Stepfamilies should work just like nuclear families.**
Reality: **The stepfamily is a different kind of family; it cannot operate in the standard traditional way.**

We've already examined several major differences in your family's structure that make it impossible for any of you to function as you did in a former, more traditional, family.

Myth: **Stepparents are cruel and insensitive.**
Reality: **Stepparents share the same human qualities other adults have.**

Fiction and fairy tales have given bad press to stepparents—especially to stepmothers, who may consequently spend too much of their energy over-compensating. The stepparent's role is a difficult one with few guidelines, and, like all parents trying to do their best, stepparents make mistakes. Unfortunately, their mistakes—the same ones any parent without information and skills might make—are magnified by other people and by stepparents themselves.

Myth: **A stepfamily is created instantly.**
Reality: **Becoming a stepfamily is a gradual, long-term process.**

All stepfamilies seem to go through certain stages—some quite difficult and chaotic—before they begin to stabilize and make a commitment to work together. (Chapter 5 examines the stages of stepfamily development.)

Chart 1

MOVING FROM UNREALISTIC TO REALISTIC EXPECTATIONS

In a stepfamily, it's important for partners to recognize unrealistic expectations and replace them with realistic ones. This chart points out the positive effects such changes can have on the feelings and outlook of all stepfamily members.

Unrealistic Expectation	*Underlying Hope*	*Resulting Feelings*
"We will all love one another."	To be a happy, harmonious family.	Guilt when love doesn't occur quickly.
"Life in our former families won't matter."	To forget the past and make a fresh start.	Isolation from each other; fragmentation of parts of ourselves.
"We'll do it better this time around."	To make up for past sadness and loss.	Disappointment in our new family when everything doesn't go smoothly.
"We will and *must* function smoothly as a family."	To present a picture of family unity to friends, families, outsiders.	Frustration and discouragement about all the differences to be resolved; defensiveness about how outsiders see us.
"Everything will fall quickly into place."	To find immediate success and happiness as a stepfamily.	Fear that new marriage is failing and that this family might end.
"Our children will feel as happy about the remarriage as we do."	To give children security and stability.	Resentment toward children for not being happier, toward one another for being somehow to blame.
"Our stepchildren will respond readily to our efforts at discipline. Discipline will not present difficulties for us as a couple."	To have a positive effect on children's lives.	Anger that comes from division about rules, responsibilities, acceptable behavior, and discipline techniques.

Realistic Expectation	Resulting Feelings
"Love may or may not develop later; what's important is to accept and respect each other."	Satisfaction and comfort among stepfamily members.
"Differences in our backgrounds will be part of our daily lives. We will all need to deal with these, and we can all grow because of them."	Connection to, and pride in, the past; optimism about enriching one another's lives in the future.
"This new family will be neither better nor worse—it will simply be different."	Excitement at the prospect of building this special family together.
"All stepfamilies have difficulties and differences to work through. Presenting a polished picture to outsiders is not important."	Relief to know others face similar problems; greater ease in working to build closeness and understanding.
"Becoming a stepfamily takes time; satisfaction comes from working together to build that family."	Confidence that we can build a strong stepfamily, satisfaction in the gradual progress we make; less discouragement when obstacles and setbacks occur.
"Children will feel confused—both happy and angry—about the remarriage; they had no choice either in the ending of their first family or in the forming of this new one."	Empathy and responsiveness in dealing with the children in our stepfamily.
"Many children, teenagers especially, will be unwilling to accept authority from stepparents. Adults won't automatically agree about how to discipline."	Less resentment or sense of threat, more patience and willingness to compromise. Interested in building relationships rather than wielding authority, in cooperating rather than competing with spouse to do this.

Myth: **All stepfamily members should and will love one another.**
Reality: **It takes time to build caring relationships.**

There is no such thing as "instant love." Time and patience are needed to build relationships in the stepfamily because everyone has suffered great losses. Trust levels are low and fears are high. No one *has to* love anyone else; but when people concentrate on respect and acceptance, warmth and friendship will in time come naturally. Sometimes love, too, will grow.

Myth: **Stepfamilies formed after a death have fewer problems than those formed after a divorce.**
Reality: **All stepfamilies face difficulties and painful feelings.**

Unresolved grief, whether the result of death *or* divorce, can get in the way of building new relationships. People have to say good-bye to *any* departed mate or parent before moving on. To have a successful remarriage, it's crucial to let go of anger and guilt in a healthy way.

Myth: **Part-time stepfamilies have it easier than full-time step-families.**
Reality: **When children live between two homes, both families experience great stress.**

As they seek a sense of belonging, adults and children alike will experience the stress that the challenges of time and transition create.

When you accept any of these myths—consciously or unconsciously—the notions and misperceptions about stepfamily living grow stronger. No doubt you can identify others. Unrealistic expectations and myths based on a lack of information almost always cause sadness and problems. The resulting disappointment can lead to defeat and possibly to another divorce.

Reaching for Reality

As you read this book, you will gain information that debunks stepfamily myths and replaces misinformation with an understanding of reality. When you know what's normal *and* possible, you can clarify your expectations and begin to build. Even if you have been stuck at a difficult stage, information and skills can help you change a cycle of seeming defeat into one of success. Awareness is the key. Education builds an awareness from which you can form realistic expectations. If you have the courage to talk about these wants and needs, they can be met—and the challenges of living in a stepfamily can be dealt with creatively.

Letting Go of the Past

Unresolved loss affects stepfamily members in different ways, handicapping new relationships at a critical time. When their children are happy, adults feel successful as parents and stepparents. When children are unhappy, adults may feel inadequate or at fault somehow, as though they caused the children to feel this way. The sadness they see in their children may threaten adults by mirroring their own unresolved feelings.

We must all mourn our losses. Grief is a healthy and normal process. Many times the messages we get about grief—that it's inappropriate or selfish, that it's weak or immature to show emotions—get in the way. If people feel embarrassed, they may suppress their sad feelings.

Denied feelings are destructive to the stepfamily. Ultimately, the feelings do come out, sometimes in unproductive, even harmful, ways. In adults, they may emerge as alcoholism, infidelity, family violence, hypochondria. In children, unresolved feelings may cause illness, school rebellion, delinquency, or phobias.

Saying Good-bye

Before you can begin to build a new family life together, you must take time to say good-bye to parts of the old life. This includes ridding yourself of feelings that keep you tied to the past.

Letting go of a marriage that is no longer good for you can be an exhausting and difficult process. Your "day in court" should mark the end of one period and the start of another. But rarely is divorce that simple. While the law provides you with the piece of paper legally severing your relationship, the real work—freeing yourself emotionally from your former spouse—must be done by you. This process of breaking a marriage's psychological ties is often called the *psychic* or *emotional divorce*. In the end, this is the divorce that really matters. And though it may seem strange to use the same term, an emotional "divorce" is equally important for someone whose marriage ended through death.

Achieving an Emotional Divorce

An emotional divorce takes time—more than most people think. And the mere passage of time is not enough: getting divorced emotionally also requires resolving feelings. No magic formula exists. Your ability to reach an emotional divorce depends on many factors: the length of the marriage, the number of children and their ages, how much anger and guilt remain, the amount of self-confidence you feel, the support you seek and receive from family, friends, and other outside sources. If it was your decision to divorce, it may take less time to resolve your feelings; you may already have worked through many of the issues before deciding to end your marriage. But many people who choose divorce never think through the issues and feelings involved. Then they find the same problems recurring in a new marriage.

If your marriage ended through a divorce you did not choose or want, or through the death of a mate, you need to move through the steps of the grieving process with great care. Your first reaction to your loss was probably denial: "This really isn't happening." Then, as you gradually accepted the reality that your marriage was over, you probably began to feel anger—first holding it in, then directing it toward others. Next, reluctant to let go, you may have started bargaining with your mate or yourself: "I'll do anything if you'll just come back." The final letting go, like the darkness before a storm, was black and depressing. From it, though, you moved toward accepting your ended marriage and began to feel free from the emotional pain that tied you to the past. Only then could you move toward personal freedom and independence.

To achieve an emotional divorce, it is essential to work through these five stages of grief: denial, anger, resistance, depression, and acceptance.[1] It is especially helpful to do as much of this grief work as possible before remarriage, because whatever unresolved mourning remains will eventually be played out in the stepfamily. Don't, however, avoid doing the work because you're already well entrenched in stepfamily living. The future of everyone in your stepfamily depends on completing breaks with the past.

Though it may seem strange to use the same term, an emotional "divorce" is equally important for someone whose marriage ended through death.

Many people get stuck in one of the stages of grief. Many, whether divorced or widowed, remarry too quickly, before they have resolved their feelings about their loss. They may wish to avoid further pain; they may hope that a new marriage will make things better, soothe the loneliness, and help them forget. The leftover grief is brought to the stepfamily. Haste to remarry, for whatever reason, is one of the prime causes of the high remarriage divorce rate.

If you suspect that you remarried too soon, without having worked through some important feelings, don't despair. Stop and take the time to do that work now—before past unfinished business damages your present relationship. Begin by recognizing the feelings that link you to your former mate. Often, there is anger, a tie that can bind two people as tightly as their wedding vows once did. Then, through the process of letting go described in the next few pages, work toward acceptance and the achievement of an emotional divorce.

These kinds of positive changes might upset your remarriage. It is wise to alert your spouse to what you are experiencing so he or she won't feel threatened. The process may unearth buried feelings that you may unconsciously project onto your new mate. If that person understands what you are going through, it will be easier to be patient and supportive. To complete the process of letting go of old feelings, you may need help from a professional family counselor. Don't hesitate to seek one out.

Unresolved grief carries two leftover feelings: anger and guilt. Each of these emotions can cause behavior that affects stepfamily relationships. Although these emotional leftovers didn't originate in the stepfamily, their presence impedes its progress.

Anger. Anger comes from your perception that you have been treated unfairly. The anger that comes with divorce reflects the rage you feel when your love relationship ends—especially when ending it was not your idea. Unresolved anger is an emotion with little positive payoff. Continuing to hold it in neither changes the past nor helps you create a better future. Anger can be expressed in negative ways such as revenge and vindictiveness; unexpressed anger can result in depression or psychosomatic problems including tension, headaches, back problems, and ulcers. *Anger toward your former spouse generally reflects the lack of an emotional divorce.*

Anger keeps people stuck in the past.

Unresolved anger dominates your thoughts and wastes precious moments as you try to build your stepfamily. Until you turn away from these unproductive feelings, you will have trouble coparenting with your former spouse. Rather than attending to the best interests of your children, you may continue to war with one another. Your unresolved relationship with a former spouse may cause problems for other members of your stepfamily. Your new mate may feel insecure or jealous. Your children will sense the strain, and loyalty conflicts will make moving back and forth between two homes difficult for them.

Guilt. Guilt is the other remnant of unresolved grief. Guilt is the feeling you have done wrong. If you perceive that you have let yourself or someone else down, you may feel bad or worthless. Perhaps you feel you did something that caused your former partner to go away. Maybe you left your marriage even though your mate did not want it to end. You may feel guilty for disrupting your children's lives. Unresolved guilt tends to damage self-concept and self-esteem. If you still harbor guilt about your former relationship, you may not be able to channel all your energies into your new one—even though you are remarried.

Guilt is self-disappointment, anguish over having failed your ideals. It is often the common denominator among stepfamily members. Stepparents may feel guilty if they left their own children behind, and suffer even greater guilt when they find they cannot love their new spouse's children as their own. Biological parents feel guilty for sharing time and resources with their spouse's children, shortchanging their own. Stepchildren who blamed themselves for their parents' break-up, or for any negative thoughts at the time of a parent's death, often feel guilty. And, although everyone may be feeling guilty, *no one* talks about it.

Both anger and guilt keep you stuck in the past. Since anger feeds on blame and resentment, the best way to get rid of it is to identify the events that caused those feelings, realize the events were growth experiences, and put to rest the blame or resentment you've been harboring. To rid yourself of guilt, you must give yourself permission to be an imperfect person who makes mistakes like everybody else. To love yourself as you are you need to discard your own demands for personal perfection.

Steps to Letting Go

If you confront guilt, anger, and other strong feelings openly, whatever emotional leftovers you have not mourned *can* be let go. Use these five steps as a guide:

1. Recognize the feeling. When a feeling emerges, don't push it away. Instead, stay with it, taking time to identify it. Close your eyes and experience it. Locate the feeling in your body. Can you attach a color or an image to it? Give the feeling a name: for example, *sadness.*

2. Express the feeling. Say aloud, to yourself or to another person, "I am feeling sad about my marriage ending."

3. Clarify the feeling. Examine the feeling further to see what's behind it. In the case of sadness, you are probably mourning the ending of something that began with joy and hope. But you may find you are also angry at your mate for leaving or dying, thus destroying your dream of marriage. You may feel guilty for having left or for being the one left alive. Clarify what the feeling really is all about, its many components: "I'm sad, mad, afraid. And I feel guilty, too."

4. Explain the feeling. As you go deeper into the feeling, you may find another reason at the core of it. Sadness about your ended marriage may have concealed anger at your mate's leaving, anger that, when recognized, may in turn have exposed deeply rooted fears of abandonment or rejection. When you can identify and explain the feeling's source, you can begin to respond with new behavior. At this point, you may even want to rename the feeling. Beneath what you once labeled sorrow, for example, may be a deep fear that can be traced to your childhood: "I felt the same way when I was a child and watched Dad and Mom fight."

5. Accept the feeling. Feelings are neither good nor bad; they just are. You are not a "good" or "bad" person because you have these feelings. None of us has constant control over what we feel from minute to minute. Realize that you're human, like everyone else in the world! When you stop judging feelings "good" or "bad," you can learn to accept them. Having accepted your own, you will find it easier to accept the feelings of others as well.

When, finally, you achieve for yourself an emotional divorce, you will experience the free feeling of leaving the loss behind you. It takes time to arrive at this point. If you're already in a stepfamily, you'll see how taking the time to resolve losses and say good-bye to parts of the past will change your attitude and behavior and affect your new relationships.

Getting the Help You Need

Our institutions are designed to help families. Too often, those who work within them are not sensitive to how stepfamilies work; they may then hinder the family's progress. But, increasingly, there are those who understand how this family is different—clergy, counselors, social workers, legal and judicial professionals, teachers—and they can help strengthen stepfamilies.

The church or synagogue is in a powerful position to help. It provides for many the rite of passage creating the stepfamily—the marriage ceremony. It also leaves its mark in other ways. The religious institution can offer great hope to the stepfamily through education, as in pre-*re*marital counseling, where clergy and laypersons can teach the importance of commitment and communication for all marriage partners. Possibly *Strengthening Your Stepfamily* is being read and discussed as part of a larger family-education program sponsored by a synagogue or church, where you are gaining the skills to move from stress to survival to strength.*

Many counselors, therapists, and social workers have made great strides toward strengthening stepfamilies. With special training, they've moved away from viewing the stepfamily as an oddity or exception, and from trying to treat it as a traditional nuclear family. They've learned what makes the stepfamily complicated and special—and that its stresses can be turned into strengths. By validating feelings, by creating an awareness of what is happening and what can be expected, and by teaching skills for helping the stepfamily deal with problems that may be occurring, these professionals are helping stepfamilies see themselves as normal. Millions of stepfamily members are learning that their feelings are not unusual, that they are not alone, and that there are actions they can take to strengthen their family.

The school can be a steadying, unchanging part of children's lives. When their families are in transition, children may see teachers as stable, important people to whom they can turn for help. Often, educators are the first to learn of a child's family crisis of death, divorce, or remarriage. They are in an ideal position to help—if they know how. Chapter 4 elaborates on how the school can be a positive influence in a stepchild's life.

---

*This is a reference to the book's umbrella program, *Strengthening Stepfamilies.* For information about the complete program contact the publisher: American Guidance Service, Circle Pines, Minnesota 55014-1796.

Those in the legal profession can help the stepfamily by becoming sensitized to its complex relationships and shortage of resources. Whatever the legal issue involved—adoption, custody, child support—the law cannot legislate love. Lawyers can suggest family mediation to allow couples to arrive at their own decisions about finances and custody arrangements. Judges need to realize that mutual agreements made by a divorcing couple will more likely be carried through than orders dictated by the courts.

Since legal professionals are only beginning to recognize the complexities of stepfamily relationships, don't assume that any and all will be informed and empathetic about your family's needs. Exercise caution in selecting legal counsel. The recommendation of a trusted friend or local social-service agency might be a good starting point.

The media influences our ideas and behavior. In the past, it has either ignored the stepfamily or portrayed it unrealistically. Although in recent years television entertainment programs have begun to include single-parent and step-family households, they have, for the most part, depicted contrived family groups that function like traditional families. These images are destructive because children compare those fictional families with their own stepfamily and wonder what's wrong. Television and radio have done better in the area of nonfictional coverage, producing documentaries and interviews about stepfamilies and those who work with them. In print, too, stepfamilies are beginning to be portrayed realistically—although with a strong focus on the difficulties. Stepfamilies can take advantage of the many educational programs and articles available. When they hear or read something they believe is *not* helpful, they can write to the broadcaster or publisher, making their feelings known.

All these external forces can affect your stepfamily in a positive way. But their potential to help begins with you—with your reaching out to teachers, clergy, friends, and relatives to tell them what kind of support would benefit your family, and to local counseling agencies to seek guidance for yourself and your family.

Reach out now. Changes are possible, but they must start with you.

Notes   1. Elisabeth Kübler-Ross described the stages of grief in her book, *On Death and Dying* (New York: Macmillan, 1969).

References   Bozarth-Campbell, Alla. *Life Is Goodbye, Life Is Hello.* Minneapolis: Comp-Care, 1982.

Einstein, Elizabeth. *New Connections: Preparing for Remarriage.* Boston: Shambhala, forthcoming.

———. *The Stepfamily: Living, Loving, and Learning.* New York: Macmillan, 1982; Boston: Shambhala, 1985.

Einstein, Elizabeth, and Linda Albert. *Stepfamily Living: Pitfalls and Possibilities.* Tampa: Einstein and Albert, 1983.

Jampolsky, Gerald G. *Goodbye to Guilt.* New York/Toronto: Bantam Books, 1985.

Kübler-Ross, Elisabeth. *On Death and Dying.* New York: Macmillan, 1969.

Paskowicz, Patricia. *Absentee Mothers.* New York: Universe Books, 1982.

Tally, Jim, and Bobbie Reed. *Too Close, Too Soon.* Nashville: Thomas Nelson Publishers, 1982.

Tavris, Carol. *Anger: The Misunderstood Emotion.* New York: Simon and Schuster, 1982.

Visher, Emily B., and John S. Visher. *Stepfamilies: Myths and Realities.* Secaucus, N.J.: Citadel Press, 1979.

Ware, Ciji. *Sharing Parenthood after Divorce.* New York: Viking Press, 1982.

Questions for Review

1. Name six factors that make stepfamilies different from traditional nuclear families. Can you think of other differences?_____

_____

_____

2. What are some losses your children or stepchildren experienced before joining a stepfamily? Of those losses, which has had or will have the greatest effect on your stepfamily?_____

_____

_____

3. What has been the hardest good-bye you've had to say concerning your former family? Have you said good-bye completely? How did you or how can you?_____

_____

_____

4. Of all the factors making the stepfamily a different kind of family, which do you believe is the most crucial to accept? Why?_____

_____

_____

5. What are some of the pluses of living in a stepfamily? List ideas both from the reading and from your own experience or thinking._____

_____

_____

6. What expectations do you, your partner, and the children have concerning your present or future stepfamily? How will you air and explore them?_____

_____

_____

7. What myths about stepfamilies have affected you? How can believing myths disrupt the formation of a stepfamily?_____

_____

_____

8. What guilt and anger do you still feel? What steps can you take to let go of these feelings?_____

_____

_____

9. What specific things can your school, church, synagogue, or community do to help rather than hinder your stepfamily? What might be some steps you could take to help such institutions play a more effective and positive role?

_____

_____

_____

Challenge to Conquer

Nine months after his wife died, Rudy married Phyllis and she moved into the home he shared with his two children. Before the wedding, Phyllis seemed to have a warm relationship with the children, especially Rudy's 11-year-old daughter Monica. Lately, Monica seems to have withdrawn. She spends a lot of time alone in her room; sometimes Rudy and Phyllis hear her crying. Yesterday, when Phyllis asked her stepdaughter to straighten up after herself in the family room, Monica screamed, "You're not my mother—leave me alone!"

1. What might Monica be thinking and feeling?_____

_____

_____

2. How might Phyllis be feeling about herself?_____

_____

_____

3. How can Phyllis and Rudy help Monica adjust? How can they help each other?_____

_____

_____

Activity for the Week

This week, take time out for beginning to get in touch with unresolved mourning issues within your family. Plan a time to be together just to talk about each person's losses. Listen intently to each other. Clarify and explain the feelings. Accept resentment and sadness as a real part of your stepfamily's beginnings. Then, before you leave for other activities, have each person tell at least two things she or he likes, or might grow to like, about your stepfamily.

Points to Ponder

- The stepfamily is a different kind of family. It is a real family and offers great possibilities for a rich family life.

- Making a stepfamily takes time — a long time. Be patient, because stability is not achieved overnight.

- Taking time to grieve the loss of your former family is important.

- Acceptance is necessary to begin the process of trust, a must for merging two separate families into one.

- The biological parent who does not live in your stepfamily is very important to your children or stepchilden. Encourage continued contact.

- Children need to move between Mom's home and Dad's. Understand that their transitions are stressful and help them feel a sense of belonging in both homes.

- Unrealistic expectations and myths are the great destroyers of stepfamily potential. Clarify your hidden agendas and expectations.

- Even though you have remarried, you may not have achieved an emotional divorce from your former spouse. Recognize this and work on letting go.

- Living in a stepfamily can offer day-to-day benefits as well as many long-term rewards for adults and children.

Understanding My Stepfamily

1. Identifying losses. In this chapter you learned how important it is to mourn the losses experienced by stepfamily members. Use the chart below to identify the specific losses for each member of your family and to determine if the mourning is finished or if further steps need to be taken.

Name of Family Member	*Loss Experienced*	*Mourning Completed?*	*Ways to Help Finish Mourning*
_____	_____	_____	_____
_____	_____	_____	_____
_____	_____	_____	_____
_____	_____	_____	_____
_____	_____	_____	_____
_____	_____	_____	_____
_____	_____	_____	_____
_____	_____	_____	_____

2. Do you have an emotional divorce? Check your progress on letting go of your old relationship by answering yes or no to the following statements:

_____ I think of my former spouse only occasionally now.

_____ I no longer become upset when I have to deal with my former spouse.

_____ I have stopped trying to please my former spouse.

_____ I no longer seek excuses to talk with my former spouse.

_____ I rarely talk about my former spouse to my friends.

_____ I have accepted that we are not getting back together.

_____ My feelings of romantic love are gone.

_____ My emotional commitment to my former spouse is over.

_____ I can accept my former spouse having a love relationship with another person.

_____ I am no longer angry at my former spouse.

Strengthening the Couple Relationship

W*e have a pact: When things get too crazy, we chuck it all, beg, borrow, or steal a sitter, and sneak off for a day in the country. We just get in the car and go. It's amazing what that time alone together—unstructured, unplanned—does for our souls! And we go back home relaxed, united—ready to cope again."*

In the stepfamily, as in any two-parent family, the strength of the couple's relationship is the key to stability. Building a strong marriage is always a challenge; for two people establishing a stepfamily, that challenge can seem overwhelming. From the start, each is juggling three roles: parent, partner, and individual. Both partners may also need to build new relationships with the spouse's children while maintaining a strong commitment to their own. The newlyweds' instant family gives them little time alone together. Balancing intimacy and romance with family responsibility and personal needs is the stepfamily couple's special, immediate challenge.

Chapter 2 provides information about stresses that can intrude on a couple's growing relationship. It explores past and present factors affecting stepfamily stability and discusses how partners can work to make their marriage thrive in this complex family environment.

Integrating the Past with the Present

In the stepfamily, the past may intrude on the present, causing stress. Children and former spouses cannot, of course, be wished away. You *can,* however, transform the past, and the relationships it included. You can change the meaning it has in your life.

Reality Reigns

Child support, alimony, shared parenthood, telephone calls, school conferences, Father's Day, Mother's Day—even a child's bone structure and coloring (so like the *other* parent's)—all are constant reminders that you or your spouse had a love relationship with someone else. Although you may find this reality unpleasant, it's best to try to accept it.

Ex means *former* and implies that something no longer exists. But an ex-spouse *does* exist, and even though the marriage may be legally over, a psychological attachment usually remains. This connection to the past needs to be accepted, so that neither partner is denying the history of a former marriage. Acceptance is important whether a prior marriage ended through divorce *or* death. In either case, denial and resistance bring pain and keep your stepfamily from moving forward.

How much you allow a former marriage to interfere in your new relationship depends on many things: the amount of time that's gone by, help you may have gotten after the marriage ended, your individual maturity, and the maturity level of your relationship. For you, individual maturity may have come through personal growth between marriage and remarriage. Your divorce or the death of your spouse may have led you to make great strides in your own personal development. As you explored your share of responsibility for the ended marriage, you probably began to see what you could have done differently, what you want to avoid repeating. You learned that you can take charge of your own life. You might also have discovered that you can change your behavior with a new mate, that you can *choose* how to respond to your present spouse, your former one, and all the other people you interact with. Rather than dreaming of what might have been—if only this were your first marriage, if only there were no ex-spouse, no children, no support to be paid—you are coming to terms with what *is*. When you stop trying to change things, let go of the idea that you can make up for the past, and accept new family members and their accompanying histories, then and only then will true commitment to making your stepfamily work become possible.

Coming to Terms with the Past

Since you cannot change the past or solve problems by ignoring its impact on your couple relationship, progress can only be made when you accept the reality of former relationships—your own and your partner's—and bring concerns and long-denied feelings out into the open.

Express and explore fears. Unexamined fears breed uncertainty in relationships. There are many possible sources of fear for stepfamily couples.

If your own relationship started during one or both of your former marriages, you may have nagging fears of continuing infidelity. Too often in a situation like this, people may have ended one marriage and moved into another without identifying, examining, and leaving behind the guilt and anger such a triangle produces. While unfaithfulness is often the impetus for first marriages breaking up, rarely is it actually the underlying cause.

"Neither of us would have gotten involved with someone else if we'd been happy together to begin with."

Infidelity is less common in remarriages[1]; still, the knowledge that a partner has had past affairs may cause feelings of insecurity.

When a former spouse has emotional or physical problems, these problems may intrude on the stepfamily. Out of guilt, you or your partner may feel the need to rescue a former mate. But, since time and money are often scarce in stepfamilies anyway, doing favors for an ex-spouse who is still emotionally hanging on to the marriage may be too costly to your remarriage. Likewise, being overly nice to stay on a former spouse's good side may cause your new partner to fear that you are not emotionally free of the other person, or that your ex-spouse is trying to win you back.

Lifestyle patterns carried over from past relationships can affect new ones. If your tastes, values, political views, or hobbies were acquired during your former marriage, your new spouse may feel competitive, jealous, and resentful. As a couple, you will need time to develop a shared lifestyle. In the meantime, fears may cause an insecure mate to worry that he or she cannot measure up to an ex-spouse. This is especially true when a deceased wife or husband has been elevated to near sainthood by friends and family.

One of the greatest fears of people in stepfamilies is that of another failure. If this marriage seems to be a replay of your first one, your commitment to the stepfamily may be weak; your remarriage may be in danger. Because family members have already experienced a great loss, their fear of failure can become acute, leading to one of two responses: Some people, knowing they can survive the pain, might again consider divorce as the solution. Others may deny problems in their current relationship.

When couples use denial as a defense, they sometimes focus instead on a child. This is *scapegoating.* In an attempt to lessen their unspoken fears that this marriage is failing, partners instead direct their energy and attention toward changing a child's behavior or emotional state. They may take the child to a counselor, hoping that if the child's problems are solved, the stepfamily will then be fine. Blaming a child appears less threatening to the couple than admitting they have problems of their own. But, in reality, scapegoating keeps them from facing fears, pinpointing sources of conflict, and getting the help *they* need to stabilize their marriage and their stepfamily.

To avoid facing their own problems, a couple may focus instead on changing a child.

Unexamined fears produce useless worries. Sometimes stepparents take the misbehavior of their stepchildren personally, believing the children dislike them. Some play questioning games:

"What if I devote myself to raising them and they reject me?"

"Can I be important in their lives?"

"Is it too late to make any difference?"

Progress can only be made when you accept the reality of former relationships—your own and your partner's—and bring concerns and long-denied feelings out into the open.

Often, stepparents take their roles too seriously, fearing the worst and putting pressure on themselves; but most do a better job than they give themselves credit for. While some stepparents fear they are failing their stepchildren, others may worry about their relationship with their own children. Or, with so much energy being directed toward child-related issues, they may fear that their couple relationship is losing its edge of excitement. When people don't take the time to examine them, these common fears can lead to guilt or produce needless pressure on a relationship.

To check how much your current marriage is influenced by a past one, explore how your choice of a new mate reflects your personal growth. Are you repeating patterns? Did you take time before this marriage to really discover what you want from life and in a life partner? Was your mate selection from choice, rather than need?

If, as you answer these questions, you realize you left much undone that could have helped make things easier, do not despair. Recognize what the tasks are and set about addressing them. Do you perhaps have unresolved issues with your former spouse? Are you really fulfilled in your work? Comfortable in your parenting? Do you have unspoken fears about aspects of your remarriage? Talk with your present spouse about your discoveries so she or he is not threatened as you clear up the past. Seek your mate's patience and support, explaining that this will ultimately strengthen your relationship. It is never too late.

Whether you're about to marry, recently married, or several months or years into stepfamily living, take the time now to talk with your partner about hidden fears. Eliminating fears won't be a simple process; you'll both need to be willing to reveal feelings to each other, to be honest about them and discuss them openly. In the process, you will be building trust on which your relationship can grow. To do this, many couples need the help of a marriage counselor or support group. Remember, all your efforts are for the benefit of your marriage and stepfamily. There couldn't be a better cause!

Examine and resolve relations with your family of origin. Ideally, the important psychological task of cutting loose from your parents will have been completed before your marriage or remarriage. If this is not the case, you may find that many of your present approaches and responses are rooted in your relationship with your first family, the one into which you were born. Problems you blamed on your former spouse may be recurring in your new marriage: you may now begin to see that you are still repeating behavior based on early ties and struggles with your parents.

We are who we are, either in harmony with our parents or in reaction to them. Childhood memories, conflicts, and feelings continue to affect all our relationships. Two negative reactions commonly carried into adulthood are the need for parental approval and the desire to banish in ourselves traits unpleasantly associated with parents. Once you begin to see that old fears, ways of thinking, or insecurities are repeating themselves in your life, you may decide to release this emotional backlog through counseling or self-help books. Two excellent books on this subject are *Making Peace with Your Parents,* by Harold H. Bloomfield and Leonard Fender, and *Cutting Loose: An Adult Guide to Coming to Terms with Your Parents,* by Howard Marvin Halpern. (For facts of publication, see "References" at the end of this chapter.) The approach you take matters less than the fact that you choose to leave negative parental influences behind you. Resolving old conflicts with parents will help reduce struggles in current relationships and may in fact be the most important investment you make for the future of your stepfamily.

It's important to understand too, though, that coming to terms with your parents may result in radical changes within you. As you leave negative feelings behind, you may disturb or confuse your mate by responding differently

As you leave negative feelings behind, your mate may find you responding to familiar situations in unfamiliar ways.

in familiar situations. This, in turn, could alter and possibly disrupt your marriage relationship. If your couple commitment is strong, however, personal growth work that helps you become a healthier person can also help strengthen your marriage.

When a former mate won't let go, change your own response. In Chapter 1 you explored ways to achieve an emotional divorce. But what if you have done so and your former mate has not? Much as you try to devote energy toward making your new family work, too often you find yourself listening to your ex-spouse's attacks or demands. As you deal with continuing letters and phone calls, you are caught between two people who feel they have an emotional claim on you. This can cause unhappiness for you and your current mate and wreak havoc in your remarriage.

Not surprisingly, it is often the spouse who chose to end the marriage who lets go and heals first. If infidelity ended the marriage, the pain is heightened for the person left behind. Because infidelity *is* traumatic, the rage and resentment that accompany it often last for years and reveal themselves in punishing behavior by the former spouse.

Hostile feelings can link two people together as strongly as their wedding vows once did. But it's vital to break that link. If your former spouse has chosen to cling to you through anger and has done little to let go of the marriage, there is nothing you can do to change that. You cannot change that person, no matter how hard you try. What you *can* do is *change the way you respond to your former spouse* until, eventually, the relationship is transformed. *You can learn to respond to old patterns in a new way.* Relationships are like wind chimes: blow on one piece and everything moves. If you change *your* behavior and responses, eventually your former mate will react differently too.

Think for a moment about the "games" you remain trapped in with your former spouse.

In the past when Consuela's former husband Martin criticized her, she would feel defensive. His put-downs reminded her of when she was a little girl and her father scolded her. To get even, Consuela would attack Martin; their battle would escalate. Now remarried, Consuela needs to learn a new response so she will no longer be affected when Martin displays this behavior. To Martin's, "With all the money I give you, the kids' clothes sure look shabby," she might respond calmly, "I'm sorry you feel that way," and finish communicating about the business at hand. Should Martin continue with the game, Consuela might simply say, "I have to go now. I hope we can settle this issue at another time. How about four-thirty tomorrow?" After a while, when Martin sees that Consuela is no longer upset, the game will cease to be rewarding to him.

Psychological games of competition require two opponents. If you simply refuse to take part in a game with your former spouse, it cannot continue. In the long run, not playing will be easier on everyone. Changing your way of responding is not simple. It takes genuine effort and practice. But it's worth the effort! Instead of investing in this dead relationship, put your energy into learning skills that can change your response. Once free of past emotional entanglements, you can redirect the energy you were using to activate your anger: you can use it creatively to build the relationship with your new spouse.

Living in the Present, Looking to the Future

When a couple marry and form a stepfamily, they face three major tasks: coping with family and children, building their marriage relationship, and continuing to grow as individuals. Each is a challenge in itself, yet the trio of tasks must be met simultaneously.

Family Matters—Making Major Decisions

Certain decisions affect the entire stepfamily. Both partners need to agree on basic issues such as how to handle money, where to live, how to discipline.

Ideally, couples will have discussed these things before the wedding. If not, it's important that they now identify problem areas and learn to either accept their present situation or begin to change it. These potential conflicts require swift resolution so they will not interfere with overall stepfamily stability. If you have serious disagreements or problems that don't seem easily reconciled, ask a counselor for help. The success of your stepfamily will be worth the investment!

Money Matters—One Pot or Two?

For better or worse, marriage creates an economic enterprise in which the couple earn, spend, and save money to build their family's future. Money can divide or unite a stepfamily—especially when it gets linked to commitment and love. The emotional commitment promised in the marriage ceremony is only a first step toward building financial commitment. Economic commitment to a new spouse may come slowly. A stepparent's commitment of resources and assets to stepchildren may come even more slowly, if at all.

 Money in the stepfamily can be managed in different ways. Although variations exist, stepfamilies tend to handle finances using either a "two-pot" or a "common-pot" approach. For many couples, when responsibilities include children and former spouses, it seems fair to keep two sets of books. This two-pot system resembles a business partnership. Sometimes lawyers are consulted and documents drawn up to protect interests. Arrangements are determined, based on past financial histories, divorce settlements, and child support. In growing numbers of dual-career stepfamilies, *he* pays for his children, *she* for hers.

Having individual control over money may reassure people that they are protected, particularly those who suffered economic hardship when their former marriage ended. This approach works less well when one partner has considerably more money than the other, or when a former spouse indulges one set of children. Under these circumstances, the stepfamily can become two subfamilies—one richer, one poorer—and bad feelings may result.

With the common-pot approach, couples pool resources and distribute them according to need, not blood ties. Adults avoid distinguishing between *yours* and *mine* and do away with extra bookkeeping. This method reflects a high level of trust and commitment to the stepfamily. Remarrieds who manage money in this way report strong family unity and a positive attitude about the future of their stepfamily.[2] But, as its name implies, the common-pot approach works only when money matters really *are* managed for the good of all.

Regardless of what approach they choose, couples must be willing to sit down together, talk over all the issues and emotions relating to money, and arrive at a specific agreement about how money matters will be handled.

Living Arrangements—Your Place or Mine?

When you remarry, you and your new spouse may each already have a house or an apartment. Deciding where to set up the combined stepfamily household is a major task.

A house is not a home, you may say. It's only a residence, a place to live. As long as we can all be together, what's the big deal about which place we choose? Don't kid yourself. Space—its allocation and adornment—defines one's identity. Someone's home reveals a lot about that person—hobbies, sports, interests, achievements.

Remarrieds who respect this reality resolve the issue before the wedding. It might seem simpler to move into one home or the other. Your decision might be based on one home's proximity to school or work. The deciding factor might be cost. But as you think about where to live, practicality is only one consideration; emotional cost is another, and it is equally important. Living in either her place or his can create problems. As the newcomers move in, some stepfamily members feel intruded upon; the rest feel like intruders. Emotional ghosts—uneasy reminders of the previous spouse—are not easily evicted. The situation can become a catch-22: changing things upsets the bereaved children, leaving things alone, the new spouse.

A fresh beginning can spare a stepfamily "space wars," while giving everyone a head start on building a positive stepfamily atmosphere. Yet sometimes a neutral move is simply not possible. When this is the case, altering the appearance and use of the space with paint, wallpaper, and some different furnishings can make a vast difference. Including children in decisions that affect their space can help ease their resentment and increase their sense of belonging.

Yours, Mine—and Ours?

To add or not to add a new baby to the stepfamily is another major decision affecting all family members. Adults may hold vastly different expectations about having another child. This is especially true if one partner has not yet had children. Having a baby is definitely a couple decision that is best settled before the remarriage; delaying this can cause couple conflict. Those who have postponed this serious decision may now need a counselor to help them unearth the reasons behind their avoidance and bring the question of having a child together into the open.

A new baby can link the two sets of family members and strengthen the stepfamily. Biologically related to everyone, this child can bring the family together. Be aware, though, that the new arrival will elicit both good and bad family feelings. Children from former marriages may feel excited about another child, or jealous and resentful, or both. And, in a stepfamily—as in any family—having a baby in order to hold together a shaky relationship is sheer folly.

The Discipline Dilemma

Until your children and stepchildren leave home, one of your main couple tasks will be dealing with discipline. This issue is important for any remarried couple with children.

The skills needed to guide children's behavior are the same for all families, but the stepfamily faces some special challenges. In stepfamilies, parents must deal with an instant family: they haven't usually had time to determine a child-rearing plan. In biological families, children and parents usually develop a close bond, so children more readily accept the parents' right to set limits and boundaries. In the stepfamily, stepchildren may reject any discipline attempts by a new stepparent.

Until children and adults have developed a rapport, most couples find it best for each biological parent to handle primary discipline issues with his or her own children. It can be made clear, however, that the stepparent has the right to discipline in the parent's absence. To achieve this interchangeable authority, the adults must share a similar approach to discipline. While a totally united front is unnecessary (all parents do not always agree on all issues), it's important that partners support each other.

To develop this support, talk together. Share your views and expectations about discipline and responsibility. Then, when one of you enforces rules with your children, the other will understand the thinking behind the behavior and be able to be supportive. Children may test you—at times to your limits! Part of that testing is to see whether they can respect you. Part, too, is to check out your adult relationship. Children need to know that a spirit of cooperation and respect exists between their parent and stepparent. As time goes on and a friendly, caring relationship with stepchildren is slowly built, the stepparent can begin to share in disciplining them. But, remember, achieving such a relationship takes time. Chapter 3 suggests additional guidelines for disciplining children in the stepfamily.

The Couple Relationship—Building Interdependence and Intimacy

Keeping a marriage exciting is hard work. In stepfamilies, it can be even more difficult. Life in a large stepfamily is complicated; sheer numbers—of people and interpersonal problems—can overwhelm even the most well-meaning couple. And, as any marriage partner knows, dreams of happiness are not magically fulfilled.

As you attempt to build your marriage, you and your partner will face several obstacles. Unrealistic or undefined expectations, poor communication, and unsatisfactory conflict resolution are three common sources of difficulties within the relationship that need to be overcome.

Expectations

Many people expect marriage to meet most of their needs: economic, emotional, sexual, and social. Their expectations about marriage arise from their beliefs about their inner needs. Few people, however, understand all their own expectations, let alone their mate's. The result? A dilemma: How can one partner meet the other's needs when neither fully understands what, in fact, those needs are?

Sometimes people remarry with unspoken contracts about unhealthy needs, such as, "You help me rear my kids, I'll help you with yours." Once the children have grown, what does the couple have left to share?

Sometimes, too, partners are too dependent on each other. Then their tight relationship creates a sense of helplessness in their children. How can a child compete with an adult for parental attention? In defense, the children may band together against the couple—or withdraw from them. In either case, the new adult will be viewed as an intruder and stepfamily unity will be low.

In the stepfamily, as in any two-parent family, the strength of the couple's relationship is the key to stability.

Similarly, distinct separateness can create distance. If both husband and wife function too independently, going their own ways and relating only to their own children, separate parent-child divisions become established. Instead of goodwill and close relations, two competitive camps form within the stepfamily. With boundaries drawn and defenses up, cooperation among stepsiblings will also be poor. Family cohesiveness cannot grow, the couple relationship deteriorates, and the stepfamily begins to falter.

Your first step, then, is for each of you to discover for yourself what needs and expectations you've brought to your marriage. Do you need physical affection? Daily time alone? Help managing the budget? The next step is to share your discoveries with each other.

You also need to examine whether expectations are realistic. Whenever a marriage is made to fill dependency needs, problems will eventually arise. Certainly, it's fair to want support and understanding. But if you expect your mate to make you happy, you are asking the impossible. While marriage can bring satisfaction and pleasure, it will not make an unhappy person happy. That is up to you. If you are depressed or chronically discouraged, seek professional help. Your spouse can support and encourage your efforts to strengthen yourself.

In order to build an intimate marital relationship within your busy stepfamily, you must work hard, understand and clarify expectations, and learn to cope with intrusions. Two people with healthy individual identities will find it comfortable to nurture and be nurtured by one another. Building this kind of interdependence takes time. A strong commitment coupled with effective communication can make it happen.

Communication

Good communication—verbal and nonverbal—involves creating understanding. How you and your spouse share your thoughts and feelings depends on many factors. Each of you has skills that evolved from your family backgrounds; one or both of you also practiced certain patterns of communication in a former marriage. Now, as you develop a style of communicating as a couple, you may be weeding out the old, destructive patterns. Or, you may find yourselves repeating those negative patterns in your remarriage.

Remarried couples who communicate well give their children a great gift. By example, and through encouraging conversation among family members, they teach their children and stepchildren skills that might never have been learned in their former families.

Some people communicate with ease. For others, expressing themselves is a struggle. Couples may need to learn skills to become better at talking with each other. Techniques such as I-messages[3] can help people express feelings without judging or blaming:

• "When I'm left to clean up alone, I feel used. It seems like you and your children think of me as a servant."

• "I feel scared when I hear so much complaining—I'm afraid if you're unhappy we might not make it together and our stepfamily will end."

Many barriers inhibit stepfamily communication. Remarrieds may have a harder time taking risks and sharing feelings that represent sadness and disappointment from former losses. If a person's history includes broken trust, lack of acceptance, or little respect, then rebuilding and learning to feel safe in a new relationship will take time. This rebuilding begins with clarifying needs and expectations within yourself, then sharing them with your mate. Talking about fears and feelings releases pent-up negative emotions and energy. That released energy can be redirected in positive ways.

As you explore the specifics of why you dislike a certain stepchild, you may learn that you dislike not the child, but her table manners. Having discovered this, you can treat that child more positively. You can begin to accept her, knowing that the irritating behavior can be changed. Later, you might want to have your mate's support to help bring about such a change. As you accept your stepchild, her resistance to you will lessen; changing the undesirable behavior then becomes easier. And, as that happens, the relationship strengthens.

Learning to recognize nonverbal messages helps you gather more information. A wink or a squeeze on the shoulder communicates affection; silence can mean lack of interest, hostility, or pain. Again, it depends on one's history.

When both partners are willing to work on learning to communicate, progress is faster. Remarried couples who communicate well give their children a great gift. By example, and through encouraging conversation among family members, they teach their children and stepchildren skills that might never have been learned in their former families.

Chart 2

SPOUSE SUPPORT FOR THE STEPPARENT

In times of anger, frustration, or discouragement, a stepparent needs the support of an understanding spouse. Simply listening and offering a kind, constructive response can make all the difference in the world.

Stepparent's Comment	*Nonsupportive Response*	*Supportive Response*
I've tried, but I just don't love your kids. I wish I could. I feel so guilty, letting you down.	You knew I had them when you married me. Love me, love my kids. So I guess if you don't love *them* . . .	It's much too soon to worry about loving them—you barely know them. I know you're trying to accept and respect them, and I'll help any way I can.
Today your son screamed at me, "I hate you! You're not my mother and I don't have to do what you tell me!"	Now don't get upset. He didn't mean it.	You must have been hurt when he was so insensitive. Apparently he's terribly upset about something. Let's try to figure out what it is.
Your kids always come back from their father's house loaded with stuff. It's not fair—how can I compete with that?	Make them take that stuff back. We don't have room for it here.	He probably feels guilty because he doesn't see the kids much. He gives them presents to make up for it. The time you spend with them means a lot more to all of us than "things."
Your ex-wife still runs your life. Whenever she calls, you jump.	Why are you so hyper? I'm married to *you,* aren't I?	I see you're upset. Can you tell me exactly what bothers you and what you'd like me to do differently?
Your daughter got into Christine's stuff again and they're fighting.	Christine does the same thing to her—she's just getting even.	Looks like we've got a case of sibling rivalry on our hands. If we're patient, they'll learn to get along—sooner or later! What can I do to help you bear with the fighting till it settles down?
I don't like it when your daughter runs around here in that bikini underwear.	You're getting upset about nothing—quit acting like a prude. We're her family, for Pete's sake!	I don't think she means any harm. We got used to being casual when we lived alone. I'll ask her to wear a robe.
I'm not going to let Dane invite your ex-husband's parents to his graduation. He hasn't seen them in months and he doesn't need to see them now. *My* parents really like Dane—*and* make an effort to see him. They're expecting to come.	They're not ex-grandparents and they're coming. Stop being so selfish. Your folks should understand how it is.	I know you're uncomfortable around them, but please try to understand how important they are to Dane. He wants them *and* your parents to come. And I'm glad your parents care enough to want to.
What do you mean you want to take your kids camping for a week? We haven't been anywhere alone since we got married.	You knew before we ever got married that my kids and I do a lot of camping.	Sounds like we need to spend more time alone together—thanks for the reminder. How about one of those hotel get-away weekends just for the two of us?

Conflict Resolution

The most important skill in the communication process is learning to resolve conflict. Conflict arises when one partner's behavior clashes with the expectations of the other. Poor communication sustains it.

Conflict between remarrieds often revolves around the children. It can also stem from unrealistic expectations and a shortage of resources in the stepfamily: stretching time and money across more than one family calls for tolerance and creativity. Other sources of difficulty might include sex, work, in-laws (current and former), religion, friends, alcohol or other drugs, and choices about leisure time. Most married couples cope with conflict in these areas, but remarried couples are especially at risk because of the greater number of people involved.

How you resolve conflict in your couple relationship will affect your entire stepfamily. When it occurs, you have three choices:

• You can choose to fight—although fighting doesn't resolve conflict. Instead, it polarizes you and your partner, dividing you with "right-and-wrong" arguments and blame games that serve to intensify rather than diminish the conflict.

Sometimes couple conflict revolves around choice of friends.

- You can deny or avoid the problem. Avoiding the issue, however, guarantees it will come up again—and again.

- You can choose to work together to solve the problem. Solving it clears the air. Learning to work through conflict brings you intimacy rather than emotional distance.

Solving conflict requires that couples take specific steps toward resolution. In their book, *Time for a Better Marriage,* Don Dinkmeyer and Jon Carlson suggest a four-step process:[4]

- **Show mutual respect.**
- **Pinpoint the real issue.**
- **Seek areas of agreement.**
- **Mutually participate in decisions.**

Consider Maggie and Will. They argue repeatedly about Will's son Brian. No matter what Maggie says or does, Brian refuses to clean his room. When Maggie appeals to her husband, he says, "Don't expect so much from the kid—he's had a lot to adjust to." "Well, so have I," replies Maggie. "And without a lot of help from you, I might add!" "Now, wait a minute," Will responds, "*I'm* just trying to keep the two of you from getting into a knock-down, drag-out fight!"

You can imagine how the argument continues; it comes up between Will and Maggie often. To begin to resolve this conflict, Maggie and Will can follow the four-step process:

1. They can show mutual respect. Will and Maggie each seem to be working to prove the other wrong. This attitude may be at the heart of their conflict. By showing mutual respect, they can open the way to seeing each other's point of view:

"When you don't back me up and tell Brian to clean his room, I feel resentful. I see you taking sides against me when I'm trying to build good habits in your son."

"I worry that you're expecting too much from Brian too soon."

2. They can pinpoint the real issue. This could be any of a number of things: Will may feel threatened by Maggie's firm stand with Brian. He may fear letting her be in charge, or worry that Brian will someday learn to respect his wife's stricter approach. For her part, Maggie may feel that she needs to assert some authority and be hurt that her husband is discounting this. She may feel unfairly treated because she's expected to discipline Brian but isn't allowed to follow her own judgment.

As Maggie and Will speak and listen to one another respectfully, they can begin to discover what the underlying issues are. Here, the problem goes deeper than whether Brian should clean his room:

"I think I hear you saying you don't want to give up control over your son."

"I guess I don't—and it seems you feel I have no faith in your judgment."

3. They can seek areas of agreement. Will and Maggie can look closely at what each is really willing to do to begin to resolve this conflict. To find a solution, of course, both will need to agree to a mutual change of behavior. But the wish to change and the decision to do so are the responsibility of each individual. Once they've agreed to cooperate rather than argue, they'll be able to search for what each can do to ease, and ultimately resolve, their conflict.

4. They can mutually participate in decisions. Here Maggie and Will can brainstorm all kinds of ideas, and begin to practice give-and-take:

Taking the time to build a strong bond with your partner does not mean you are depriving your children; indeed, building that bond is as important for your children's well-being as it is for yours.

"I could agree not to nag Brian so often or expect so much if you'll be willing to sit down with me and make a list of what we can expect of him."

"I think a list is too formal and threatening. But I'm willing to talk it through with you. Once we agree on something, we can all three sit down together and talk about it."

"But how will we get Brian to stick to an agreement?"

"Maybe we could ask Brian how he thinks that could be handled . . . He might have a few ideas of his own."

"I'm still worried that he'll want to find the easy way out and that, when he does, you'll be too lenient."

"Then let's try to agree ahead of time how to handle that, too."

Of course, resolving a marriage conflict isn't as easy as one-two-three-four! But these steps provide a framework partners can follow. As you and your spouse work to find solutions, keep the four steps in mind. If you get stuck, refer back to them.

Love alone doesn't conquer all. Marriage takes work. Anger is normal in any marriage, so when conflict arises in yours, don't panic and fear your stepfamily is failing. Conflict is one of the many challenges you and your mate will face. How you resolve it depends on how willing you both are to restore harmony to your relationship. This willingness is part of your commitment to one another.

To work on improving communication and problem-solving skills, you might want to read self-help books or join a couples' group. A special set of activities to help bring stepfamilies closer together has been developed for use with this book: the *Stepfamily Encouragement Packet.**

Taking Time to Grow

One of the most rewarding challenges you face as a couple is creating a new home with a warm, happy atmosphere that brings everyone together. In the beginning, life in the stepfamily seems like a three-ring circus. As you balance your time between building a family, caring for your personal needs, and creating a solid marriage, you become masters at juggling resources and relationships. Too often, your couple relationship gets shortchanged. Your

---

*These home activities for strengthening your stepfamily are available from the publisher, American Guidance Service.

If all your energy is directed toward children and their needs, your marriage won't have a chance to take root and grow.

instinct and need may tell you to take time for each other; your guilt about the children or concern about money may keep you from doing so. The balance is tricky. You must constantly choose between family activities and time alone as a couple.

It is critical that you understand the importance of making your couple relationship a priority. If you do not nourish your marriage, you may not stay together. A major reason for divorce among remarried couples is that the wife and husband fail to spend enough time working to build their relationship. With the focus immediately and constantly on the children and *their* needs, the marriage never has a chance to take root and grow. It may end needlessly, and then *everyone* suffers. Even if your marriage does not end, your stepfamily cannot stabilize until your couple relationship does. Until children feel that your marriage relationship is solid, they may remain withdrawn from stepparents, afraid to trust. Taking the time to build a strong bond with your partner does not mean you are depriving your children; indeed, building that bond is as important for your children's well-being as it is for yours.

Personal Growth—Taking Time for Yourself

Just as stepfamily success requires that partners work on their couple relationship, a good partnership can only exist between two people who feel complete, who have had the opportunity to grow and to realize their individual potential. A successful remarriage takes two happy, healthy people who are content with themselves.

Sometimes partners reach an impasse in building a stepfamily because they are at different places in their lives. One may be ready to spend more time outside the couple relationship while the other wants more togetherness. Or one may require a relationship of harmony while the other prefers to express and air disagreements. If couples can see individual growth and differences not as threats but as enrichments of the relationship, they can be compatible and share goals.

Continued personal growth after remarriage is essential. A balance of family, couple, and independent time is important for both partners because it provides satisfaction, good feelings, and a sense of competence. These sources of self-esteem are especially vital to stepparents, who may find helping rear someone else's children difficult and most rewards long-term.

Chaos and confusion, complex relationships, complicated schedules as children move between two homes, the constant challenge of juggling past and present relationships and carrying out your many roles: all this can make you wonder how you'll ever meet your own needs. Where will you find solitude to regain your perspective and calm your frazzled nerves? Everyone needs the luxury of time alone to think, sort, and dream. And, beyond this, if you are caught up in a difficult situation with a stepchild, you must take time alone to resolve your feelings and figure out what to do. Just as you find time for household chores, errands, or the evening news, so too can you find the time for yourself in your busy routine.

One day, when you can view your remarriage as a success, it will be easy to say, "How could I have doubted?" But it is now, while you are trying to cope with so much, that you have to give yourself the time and space you need. For it will be in that circle of quiet that you will begin to gain confidence, to accept your stepchildren and yourself, to remind yourself of those possibilities you can change into realities. It is from that calm place which you have created that you will begin, once again, to trust yourself.

What's Special about Your Relationship?

Like any marriage, a successful remarriage is not a matter of chance. At times, as you struggle, you may even regret you were unable to keep your former marriage together: "If I only knew then. . . ." To succeed now, you know you need skills in communication and conflict resolution. But, above all, as a couple you must have a deep commitment to building and enriching your marriage. Without this strong commitment, no marriage can thrive. With it, you have the power to make choices and control what happens in your stepfamily. When you commit yourselves to seeing how your differences add to, rather than subtract from, your marital satisfaction, you can begin to build a positive foundation for your family.

As you work at this marriage, focus on its strengths, on the qualities that attracted you to each other in the first place. These can be a beacon, lighting the way for you to create a positive environment for building the future.

Notes

1. Glynnis Walker, *Second Wife, Second Best?* (New York: Doubleday, 1984).

2. Barbara Fishman and Bernice Hamel, "One Pot or Two," *Stepfamily Bulletin* (Spring 1983).

3. Thomas Gordon, *Parent Effectiveness Training.* (New York: Thomas H. Wyden, 1970).

4. Don Dinkmeyer and Jon Carlson, *Time for a Better Marriage* (Circle Pines, Minn.: American Guidance Service, 1984).

References

Bloomfield, Harold H., and Leonard Felder. *Making Peace with Your Parents.* New York: Random House, 1983; New York: Ballantine, 1985.

Campbell, Susan M. *Beyond the Power Struggle.* San Luis Obispo, Calif.: Impact Publishers, 1984.

————. *The Couple's Journey.* San Luis Obispo, Calif.: Impact Publishers, 1980.

Crosby, John F. *Illusion and Disillusion: The Self in Love and Marriage.* Belmont, Calif.: Wadsworth Publishing, 1976.

Curran, Doris. *Traits of a Healthy Family.* Minneapolis: Winston Press, 1982.

Davitz, Lois Leiderman. *Baby Hunger.* Minneapolis: Winston Press, 1984.

Dinkmeyer, Don, and Jon Carlson. *Time for a Better Marriage.* Circle Pines, Minn.: American Guidance Service, 1984.

Einstein, Elizabeth. *The Stepfamily: Living, Loving, and Learning.* New York: Macmillan, 1982; Boston: Shambhala, 1985.

Erikson, Erik. *Childhood and Society.* New York: W. W. Norton, 1950.

Halpern, Howard Marvin. *Cutting Loose: An Adult Guide to Coming to Terms with Your Parents.* New York: Simon and Schuster, 1976; New York: Bantam Books, 1983.

Mace, David. *Enriching Your Marriage.* Waco, Tex.: Word, 1980.

Paul, Jordan, and Margaret Paul. *Do I Have to Give Up Me to Be Loved by You?* Minneapolis: CompCare, 1983.

Sager, Clifford J., Hollis Steer Brown, Helen Crohn, Tamara Engel, Evelyn Rodstein, and Libby Walker. *Treating the Remarried Family.* New York: Brunner/Mazel, 1983.

Walker, Glynnis. *Second Wife, Second Best?* New York: Doubleday, 1984.

Questions for Review

1. In what ways do unrealistic expectations affect your stepfamily? The individuals in your stepfamily? Your couple relationship?_____

_____

_____

2. What are some ways fears from the past can jeopardize your couple and stepfamily relationships?_____

_____

_____

3. What steps can you take to come to terms with the past?_____

_____

_____

4. What is *scapegoating* in the stepfamily? How does it happen and where does the real problem usually lie?_____

_____

_____

5. How does resolving issues with your parents affect your role as spouse or stepparent?_____

_____

_____

6. What loyalty conflicts do adults in the stepfamily face?_____

_____

_____

7. What are some major family decisions stepfamily couples face?_____

_____

_____

8. What do you think is the best way for stepfamily couples to handle finances? Why?_____

_____

_____

9. Is adding an "ours" baby to the stepfamily wise? Please discuss._____

_____

_____

10. What reasons might a couple have for not revealing hidden agendas or clarifying expectations about remarriage before the wedding? Based on your reading of this chapter, how would you counter those reasons?_____

_____

_____

11. How can communication be a major source of stress? How can partners improve communication and reduce this stress?_____

_____

_____

12. What are some areas of conflict most stepfamily couples face? How can you work to resolve conflict in your marriage?_____

_____

_____

13. What three relationship tasks must adults in the stepfamily handle simultaneously? Which task needs to take priority? Why?_____

_____

_____

14. Do you believe it is selfish to take time for yourself, away from your spouse and stepfamily? Explain your answer._____

_____

_____

Challenge to Conquer

Lou's former spouse, Ed, seems to be the center of many conflicts in her remarriage. He uses the children to get little extras from Lou, writes nasty notes, and puts down her new husband Paul's efforts to establish warm relationships with the children. This behavior upsets Paul, and often Lou feels caught between the two men.

1. What might Ed be thinking and feeling?_____

_____

_____

2. What might Paul be thinking and feeling?_____

_____

_____

3. Can Lou change Ed's behavior or Paul's reaction to it? What can she do to change the situation?_____

_____

_____

Activity for the Week

Take two sheets of paper, one for you and one for your partner.

Each of you is to write the numbers 1-20 down the side of your own sheet. Then, as quickly as you can, without censoring and in no special order, list 20 things you love to do with your partner.

After both lists of 20 are completed, code your responses, using the following symbols. Place the symbols to the left, just before the activity numbers.

$ Place a dollar sign **($)** by each activity that would cost money.

P Place a **P** by each activity that, for you, is more fun with other people in addition to your partner.

A Place an **A** by those activities you prefer to enjoy alone as a couple.

5 Put a **5** on any activity that might have been on your list five years ago.

* Place an asterisk **(*)** in front of each of your five favorite activities.

+ Place a plus sign **(+)** next to those activities you believe your partner loves best.

Record before each entry the date on which you last did that activity together.

Share your completed lists with one another, discussing the similarities and differences between them. Together, create one master list, representing a composite of both your preferences. Spend some time discussing your discoveries and present feelings.*

---

*Adapted from Sidney B. Simon, Leland W. Howe, and Howard Kirschenbaum, "Twenty Things I Love to Do," from *Values Clarification* (Glenview, Ill.: Scott-Foresman, 1980).

Points to Ponder

- Your couple relationship sets the tone for the rest of your stepfamily.

- Clearing up unfinished emotional business with your parents and former spouse will enrich your remarriage.

- Decisions about financial problems affect stepfamily unity, so creative solutions are required.

- Stepfamilies who set up their households in a new neutral environment avoid many problems.

- An "ours" baby can either link your two families or cause stepfamily members, especially children, to feel threatened.

- Three tasks stepfamily couples face are coping with family and children, building their marriage relationship, and continuing to grow as individuals.

- A strong couple relationship requires that the two people clarify expectations, build communication and conflict-resolution skills, and have a deep commitment to making their marriage work.

Understanding My Stepfamily

For you and your partner to benefit most from this activity, first complete it individually and then share your responses with one another. Together, identify and discuss the similarities and differences in your answers.

1. How much is my current marriage influenced by my past one? Answer the following questions as objectively as you can:

• When something—positive or negative—brings to mind my ex-spouse, do I overreact? If so, in what ways?_____

_____

_____

• How is my new partner different from or similar to my former one?_____

_____

_____

• Does my present behavior duplicate in any way past behavior toward my former spouse? How? When I behave in this way, what response do I hope for from my new mate?_____

_____

_____

2. Clarifying expectations. The couple relationship is strengthened when each person knows the expectations of the other and differences are negotiated to reach a compromise. Use the following list of stepfamily issues as a springboard for such discussions with your mate. Check the items you feel have not been sufficiently discussed and clarified. Then write down your expectations about each of these items.

• **Career commitments and priorities.** Will both of us be able to keep our jobs and manage the extra child-care duties? How will child care be handled if both of us work outside the home? What about household responsibilities?

• **Money.** Who will pay for what? Will the family finances be treated as a common-pot venture or will separate accounts be kept? How will child support be handled?

- **Roles.** How will each of us relate to our stepchildren? What rights and duties do we have toward them?

- **Love.** How will we strengthen our love? How will we communicate our feelings? How often will we spend time together without the children? What are our emotional and sexual expectations?

- **Children.** Who will discipline whom? What are each of our rights and duties towards our stepchildren? Should we have an "ours" baby?

3. What's special about our relationship? Sit back, close your eyes, and think of all the happy events you and your spouse have shared. What special skills do you each bring to the remarriage? What special traditions or rituals have you created together? What difficult situations have you overcome successfully? After you have cleared your mind to let the joys and successes flow in, jot them all down, no matter how insignificant they may seem. Share this list with your spouse.

_____

_____

_____

_____

_____

_____

_____

_____

_____

CHAPTER 3

Creating Effective Roles and Relationships

T*he hardest thing I had to do as a stepparent was learn to listen—with my ears, eyes, mind, and heart—to what my husband and stepchildren were saying. I knew if I gave it time they would tell me where and how I'd fit into their lives."*

The most challenging role many of us will ever play—that of a parent—is often the one we are least prepared to fill. This is doubly true for a stepparent, who takes on a task that is largely undefined and filled with inherent challenges. The rewards of this task are, for the most part, long-term. Often, too, being a successful spouse conflicts with being a successful stepparent. Little wonder that, instead of excitement about becoming a new parent, many people feel apprehension about the decision to help rear another person's children. Yet each year hundreds of thousands of people remarry and agree to become stepparents.

This chapter explores the challenging task of becoming a stepparent and examines ways to define the role in order to begin building trust. Success depends on taking time to develop relationships slowly so that new bonds can be formed and strengthened.

Effective Stepparents

Although each stepfamily has a unique structure, all can be guided by the same basic principles that produce well-adjusted children and effective parents in any family. Like effective parents, effective stepparents possess certain specific characteristics:

An effective stepparent is able to empathize. When you can perceive life as another sees it, you are exercising *empathy*. Empathy isn't the same as pity or sympathy. And having been in a similar situation doesn't automatically make a person able to empathize. To empathize, one needs to look at things from the other person's point of view, as though seeing the world through the same pair of eyeglasses.

Can you enter your stepson's world of feelings and experience them in the same or a similar way? Can you feel the tug of your stepdaughter's loyalty conflict? Can you sense the sadness and loss that might overwhelm your stepchildren? Can you imagine any reasons why they might be hostile or indifferent to you?

You are practicing empathy when you can honestly say, "If I were in those shoes, I'd feel the same way." The more you're able to feel empathy toward your stepchildren, the more you will understand them and the better your chances of becoming a successful stepparent.

An effective stepparent is not defensive. Blaming, taking sides, and showing favoritism are reactions to a perceived threat. Each of these responses is defensive. As your stepchildren test the limits and boundaries of their new relationship with you, comparing you with their absentee parent or blaming you for their loss of that parent, can you keep from reacting defensively?

Most comparisons or attacks aren't really directed at you. Rather, they usually represent the children's need to defend their biological parent or reflect their loss and sadness.

When an angry stepchild screams, "I hate you—you're not my mother!" an unthreatened stepparent will empathize with the child and explore the feelings behind the behavior. The child may really be wondering, "If I learn to care about you, will you leave me too?" or, "Will you take my mom away from me?"

The basis for remaining nondefensive is respect. When you can respect your stepchild's right to feel all feelings deeply, without defending yourself or counteraccusing, you both benefit. You might say, "I don't expect you to agree with the way I do everything, but I do ask that you respect my point of view and feelings. And I'll respect yours."

An effective stepparent avoids being judgmental. We are all guilty of judging at times, even when we don't mean to do so. Often judging may be subtle. You might tell your spouse, "My kids never do that," implying that your way is right, your mate's wrong. To your stepchild, you might say, "If you'd just use your head!"—implying that the child is either stupid or wrong. When you resist evaluating your stepchild negatively, you'll be on your way to building a positive relationship with that child.

An effective stepparent shows acceptance. The cornerstone of good relationships with stepchildren is acceptance. Again, respect is the key. As an accepting stepparent, you respect children regardless of their behavior. You relate to stepchildren as equals without setting conditions or insisting on changes to fit your way of doing things. You respect your stepchildren's ability to conduct their own lives, to make decisions, and to take responsibility for themselves. You also respect the history of their former families and their need and right to continue an ongoing relationship with both their biological parents.

An effective stepparent is open to change. The stepfamily results from a reorganization of the family system. These changes and transitions call nearly everything into question. Beliefs and behaviors are scrutinized. Skills are tested. Requests are resisted. While change often includes crisis, it's your response to the crisis that counts. Remaining rigid or closed to trying things differently will create more opposition.

Effective stepparents see change as a challenge, a chance for growth. If they do not fear that growth, their entire stepfamily relaxes. When met with enthusiasm and expectancy rather than resistance and fear, change can enrich your stepfamily.

An effective stepparent has a strong sense of personal identity. Since stepparents routinely encounter stressful situations, a successful stepparent needs a strong, positive self-image, a powerful sense of personal value. Self-confidence and self-respect, the main components of self-esteem, add up to this sense of personal worth.

A positive outlook can ease everyone's adjustment.

Self-esteem also includes self-acceptance. It's so important to have the courage to be imperfect, to accept yourself with all your faults and limitations. As you try to carve out a role with your stepchildren, you will make mistakes and meet setbacks. To withstand the pressures brought on by such setbacks, it is important that you feel positive about yourself. Only when you recognize yourself as a separate person, sure of your identity, will you be able to allow others in your stepfamily to be individuals too.

An effective stepparent believes in children's abilities and allows them to be responsible for themselves. You are responsible *to* your step-children, not *for* them. You do not take responsibility for your stepchildren's habits or attitudes, developed long before you became involved in their lives. You do not overcompensate for the pain they have experienced or feel you must make up for lost time. Remember, rather than sympathize, you can empathize. Like you, your stepchildren are in the process of becoming. You can meet them where they are and discover how you can fit into their lives in a positive way.

Chart 3A
STEPPARENTING ROLES

The contrast between a misguided and an effective approach to stepparenting provides a key to success in the stepfamily. Clearly, the effective stepparent works with accurate information and chooses specific behaviors to build toward positive relationships.

Misguided Stepparent

Tries to replace the absent parent
- Feels insecure about stepparent role
- Wants to own children and their affections
- Attempts to cut ties with noncustodial parent
- Assumes children cannot love several adults
- Creates loyalty conflicts for children

Demands love and acceptance
- Expects to care about stepchildren immediately
- Expects children to express affection right away
- Feels guilty when children express affection they don't really feel

Insists feelings for stepchildren and biological children are the same
- Tries to deny rather than accept differences in feelings
- Feels guilty for loving own children more
- Overcompensates with stepchildren by giving gifts, spending extra time, expressing phony feelings

Manages everyone else's relationships
- Takes on problems of all family members as own
- Interferes in communication efforts of siblings, kids, biological parents
- Keeps family members from forming direct relationships with one another
- Insists on being included in activities
- Deprives parents and children of needed private time and space together

Assumes peacemaker role
- Fears another family loss
- Believes difficulties imply failure
- Denies problems exist
- Shuts out negative emotions
- Reacts defensively when stated feelings and real feelings clash

Strives to be perfect and thus counteract "wicked stepparent" myth
- Allows no imperfection in self as parent figure
- Avoids mistakes at all costs
- Suppresses negative emotions
- Refuses to state any opinions that might create conflict

Feels sorry for children of loss
- Tries to make up for children's parental loss
- Pities children and delays grieving process necessary to heal
- Indulges, pampers, and therefore prevents stepchildren from learning to understand life as it really is with its pain and adversities

Insists on family unity
- Views goal as happiness and harmony at all costs
- Uses family "togetherness" to show outsiders "how great we're doing"
- Dictates activities and denies free choices among family members
- Diverts family members from preferred activities

Effective Stepparent

Recognizes importance of noncustodial parent
- Respects children's need and right to love that parent
- Helps stepchildren nurture relationship by encouraging them to write, phone, visit
- Allows picture, mementos of biological parent without creating conflict
- Invites parent to important milestone ceremonies and events
- Strives to be added parent figure and friend rather than substitute parent

Acknowledges existing bond between new spouse and children
- Realizes it's natural to feel closer to biological children
- Reduces jealousy and competition for time and attention
- Controls resentment when child and parent need time alone

Allows time for relationships to develop
- Focuses on process of developing as a family unit
- Values each small success as evidence of relationship growth
- Minimizes worrying or trying to force progress
- Respects and accepts others as new family forms

Manages own relationships with each child
- Avoids interfering in other people's problems unless invited
- Encourages family members to care for own needs and relationships

Understands family life cannot always be happy
- Accepts that problems exist
- Understands that unhappy experiences teach children coping skills
- Allows full expression of emotions whether negative or positive, pleasant or unpleasant

Possesses the courage to be imperfect
- Rejects fairy-tale myths and unrealistic media portrayals of stepfamilies
- Understands every mistake does not reflect cruel-stepparent image
- Realizes the way people learn is by making mistakes, thinking about them, and trying again
- Shares own mistakes to give children permission to be imperfect and human

Accepts grief and loss as part of life's experience
- Encourages children to face the reality of death or divorce that preceded stepfamily
- Feels empathy, not sympathy, with children of loss
- Helps kids confront and express feelings that grief elicits
- Provides strength and encouragement so children can move into the future

Lets go
- Permits children to belong to two families with a minimum of fuss
- Allows children to spend time with peers, activities, other parent, without fearing stability of stepfamily is threatened
- Plans family activities without forcing participation
- Uses time away from children to enhance relationship with spouse

Adapted from Elizabeth Einstein and Linda Albert, "Pitfalls and Possibilities," one of four booklets in The Stepfamily Living Series *(Ithaca, N.Y. and Tampa, Fla.: Einstein and Albert, 1983), 14-16.*

Redefining Roles

Most people about to remarry don't view their role realistically. They think they'll work into it. The problem with this notion is there is no transition between becoming a spouse and becoming a stepparent. It happens as the marriage vows are shared, and the simultaneous roles often conflict.

In coping with their anxiety, many new stepparents seem to approach their role as either a Super Stepparent or a Reluctant Stepparent. The Super Stepparent rushes headlong into making the relationship work, often pressuring children who need time to deal with all the changes they've been through. The Reluctant Stepparent holds back and avoids building relationships with stepchildren, causing the natural bond between the biological parent and children to tilt the family into a power struggle.

An effective stepparent recognizes that neither of these approaches creates unity for the stepfamily or fosters close relationships. To succeed as a stepparent, a person needs more than crossed fingers and good intentions: she or he needs information and clear guidelines.

Stepparents can relate to stepchildren in several possible ways. You probably have your own ideas about what you are or are not willing to be to these children. Stepchildren have their ideas about your role too. It is important that somewhere along the line you and your stepchildren clarify your separate expectations.

Stepparents who define their role as that of friend are usually the most satisfied and successful.

Stepparent as friend. To create friendship from the arranged relationship between stepparent and stepchild isn't always easy. Yet, stepparents who define their role as that of friend are usually the most satisfied and successful.[1]

Children already have a father and a mother; this is true even if one of those parents has died or has never been known to the child. When they have continued contact with their biological parents, children usually do not need stepparents for general psychological survival. Yet in the role of friend, a stepparent can provide additional caring and concern.

Becoming a friend to a stepchild is not the same as being a buddy, and it does not mean that you have to get along perfectly all the time. An adult can be a friend who supports and empathizes with a stepchild's complex feelings. Offering friendship is far less threatening than coming in to take over. When you build your role from the basis of friendship, you give children time to come to know and respect you.

Stepparent as confidant. A stepparent gives children another adult sounding board. This is especially important for teenagers, who sometimes feel alienated from their parents and uncomfortable seeking their advice.

The normal assertiveness and turbulence of adolescence often cause stressful relationships between parents and their teenage children. Offering other options and opinions, a supportive stepparent can soften the sharp edges of a child's relationship with the parent of the same sex. Stepparents must be careful, of course, not to develop an alliance with the child against the other parent or to allow themselves to be used to hurt the other parent.

The role of confidant allows a stepparent to become an adviser. As you transmit values and beliefs to your stepchildren, you can feel good about yourself. When both adults are doing this for each other's children, everyone's life is enriched.

Stepparent as another parent figure. If your stepchildren are very young or have little contact with their noncustodial parent, you might be considered as a primary parent, another parent. The key here is to understand that *another* means *in addition to* rather than *a replacement for.*

It is important to treat your children and your stepchildren alike; that is, to have similar expectations of and respect for them. But being another parent does not mean you must *feel* the same about them. Stepparents who serve as another parent figure in the lives of their stepchildren too often get their own needs mixed up with those of the children they are parenting. Being a primary parent to your stepchildren can open you to many hurts if you become so emotionally attached to these children that you try to deny they have another parent somewhere.

Stepparent as mentor. A mentor's role is teaching, consulting, sharing expertise and information that may help prepare another person for life. Beyond their parents, children need special people in their lives, passing on skills, knowledge, and wisdom. Such a person might be a teacher, a Scout leader, or perhaps a next-door neighbor.

Many stepchildren say their stepparent played an important role as their teacher or mentor. A mentor, however, is not a meddler. Before you begin, be sure your stepchildren want your expertise.

Stepparent as role model. The stepparent as mentor teaches a certain child a specific skill; the child learns consciously and willingly. The stepparent as role model teaches by setting an example; here the child learns unconsciously and copies the behavior of the stepparent. An additional adult in the family provides another close-up model for stepchildren, giving them a new way of trying on life and viewing the world. Thus, what starts out as a problem in the stepfamily—too many differences—becomes an opportunity!

As a stepparent, you may fit one or more of the categories. Depending on your stepchildren's needs and your own, you might shift from one role to another. What is critical is that you and your partner make a conscious choice about the stepparent role in your children's lives. From choice, specific goals can be set. While input from the children is important, couples must make the final decision about which role the stepparent is to play.

The Shape of Your Stepfamily

As a stepparent, your perspective and problems will depend on your basic stepfamily configuration. Is it full-time or part-time? To whom do the children belong?

The Stepfamily with Children from One Partner Only

Being a biological parent is challenge enough; beginning parenthood as a stepparent is even harder. Not only are you adjusting to your partner, you are adjusting to being a parent at the same time.

Of all the stepparent roles, that of the stepmother with no children of her own is often the hardest.[2] Having no experience rearing children, she receives no validation as a parent—from her spouse or her society. Male or female, step-parents thrust into the role of primary caregiver must often cope both with the unrealistic expectations of spouse and in-laws and with stepchildren who can be unappreciative and unpleasant as they try to adjust. Little wonder that many stepparents feel like failures in their first efforts at being parents. "If this is what it's like to be a parent," they may reason, "I don't want children of my own."

Such thinking can be avoided. There's another point of view! Being a stepparent before you are a parent presents an especially rigorous training ground—one that might even make you a *better* parent. Many people in this position report that once they have their own child they feel good about their parenting skills. With the pressure lowered and a renewed confidence in themselves, they become better stepparents.

Stepparents with no children of their own needn't cope with the guilt of leaving children behind. Instead, for many, their major difficulty is to figure out how to belong—how to become a significant part of the existing family.

Instant parenthood brings unexpected challenges.

Many a stepparent is welcomed with open arms—by a spouse who is glad to have a partner in parenting, by stepchildren who are comforted to see their parent happy and pleased to have another adult around. Stepparents who've never had families of their own may come to the role with enthusiasm about sharing skills and special times with their stepchildren. When, slowly, they befriend the children, keeping their expectations low and acknowledging the relationship the children have with their other parent, stepparents can play a significant role in the lives of their stepchildren.

Sometimes, however, a stepparent faces resentment and defiance from step-children and defensiveness from his or her new mate. The children may resent this person's taking up their parent's time; they may resist the stepparent's efforts at discipline. When a new stepparent responds to a spouse's request to help with discipline, the spouse may then turn around and defend the chil-dren! Such triangles made up of parent, child, and spouse can create big problems.

Fitting into the new family is made more difficult for the stepparent by the strong bonds formed between the biological parent and children during sin-gle-parent living, when a tight family unit was required for survival. After remarriage, the parent needs to relax these bonds and begin to let the step-parent in. She or he needs to relinquish control, time, space—the whole way of doing things without another adult in the house. If the connection between the biological parent and children remains too strong and the couple fails to

A stepparent can easily feel like an intruder.

negotiate major issues, the building of necessary stepfamily ties will be inhibited.

Stepparents walk a tightrope between respecting the existing family relationships and trying to become part of them. There are three common outcomes:

1. Stepparents take on the routines and rituals of the existing single-parent family and become integrated into the family.

2. Stepparents take control.

3. The process of change creates a new family status: the needs, wants, and wishes of all stepfamily members are taken into account as the family evolves to a new, stable place.

An unfortunate fourth possibility is that the stepparent might be driven away, branded as unsatisfactory and unable to meet anyone's expectations. Most often these unmet expectations are rooted in hidden agendas about what role the stepparent is to play.

To reduce a stepparent's feeling of being an intruder, the couple needs to explore these agendas to the extent that they are known. Only when the biological parent lets the stepparent know what place he or she hopes the spouse will play in the children's lives can the stepparent truly become an effective part of the family.

Most stepparents do a better job than they think. Most stepparents do a better job than they think. A researcher[3] compared children growing up with biological fathers to those reared by stepfathers and found that the stepchildren were just as happy and adjusted as the children in traditional families. The children said so; their mothers said so: yet the stepfathers rated their stepchildren as less happy and themselves as less effective than the biological fathers did. More conscious of their role, stepparents tend to be more critical of themselves.

In any stepfamily where only one spouse brings children to the marriage, no balance exists, no trade-offs. One chose and married a partner; the other gained a whole family. With no way to reciprocate for what the stepparent does for the children, the biological parent may feel guilty. Worse, she or he may have difficulty understanding why the stepparent is having trouble and thus fail to support the spouse in that role. Research shows that a stepparent's most important need is strong support from the biological parent, his or her new spouse. If this spouse can empathize and show appreciation, the stepparent's self-esteem will be enhanced. Thus encouraged, the stepparent will gain confidence and be more successful as a partner *and* a stepparent.

In the stepfamily with children from one partner only, the biological parent may have a relatively easier time adjusting. This person doesn't have to get used to someone else's children or become an "instant parent." If you have children and your partner doesn't, your important task is to be sensitive to integrating your new spouse into your existing family. Understanding that the stepparent's role is not an easy one, you can offer support and encouragement. It is important to express your appreciation, provide helpful feedback, and listen to what your partner is saying about feelings relating to your children.

The Stepfamily in Which Both Adults Are Parents

When both adults bring children to the remarriage, similarities may smooth the merger. Empathy creates understanding. Partners are in the same situation: each is a parent; in most cases each has or had a former spouse with whom (in the case of divorce) it is necessary to interact for the sake of the children; and each must learn to relate to the other's children. These common denominators often make it easier to offer one another support.

But children can also become dividers. Adults in the dual role of biological parent and stepparent may feel like jugglers, developing new relationships with their partner's children while nurturing existing ones with their own. If the couple have not united in their expectations and are not tending their marriage, their children can come between them. Two armed camps then develop. When this occurs, everyone loses. As parents rush to the defense of their respective children, their couple relationship deteriorates. As the chil-

---

Guidelines for Easing the Adjustment to Stepfamily Living

For stepparents:

• Seek support—from your spouse, friends, minister or rabbi, other stepparents.

• Be there for your stepchildren, but allow them time to learn to trust and respect you.

• Respect the strong bond that exists between your spouse and the children. Allow them plenty of time together and avoid interfering where issues are not your concern.

For biological parents:

• Include your new spouse in your existing family unit, but let relationships develop at their own pace.

• Be supportive, ready to listen and discuss difficulties.

• Encourage a cooperative spirit between your spouse and the children's other biological parent.

For both of you:

• Explore your parenting styles and take classes together to develop problem-solving and discipline skills.

• Work out ways for your stepfamily to communicate: family meetings, bulletin boards, complaint and compliment pots, regular planned activities.

• Talk about feelings. Airing them aloud diminishes their power.

• Be patient, allowing plenty of time for family members to work through their many differences.

• Make your couple relationship a priority. Remember, when parents are happy, children feel more secure.

dren feel the marriage coming apart, they react fearfully and begin to misbehave. Growing ties between stepsiblings loosen, rifts widen, and everyone gets edgy.

Guilt becomes the common bond in the stepfamily. Parents who live with their biological children only part-time feel guilty about time spent with their stepchildren. The more they enjoy the stepchildren, the guiltier they feel about rearing someone else's kids rather than their own.

When children spend only summers or weekends with a parent, that parent's guilt provokes certain behavior. Some parents overcompensate with time and money, trying to make up for not being with the children more often. As relationships become strained, guilt increases. Time with the children may become so painful that the parent chooses to see less and less of them.

Remarried people who receive little financial support from former spouses may feel grateful for the help their new spouse gives them, but also guilty about it. And children who still blame themselves for their parents' divorce may feel guilty when they hear their parent and stepparent fighting. Are they to blame again? they wonder.

Stepfamily Struggles

Stepfamily success can be sidetracked by a variety of challenges, all of which come about when expectations clash with reality, creating confusion for couples and children alike.

The Need to Be Noticed

Most stepparents today are well-intentioned people trying to counteract negative social images by becoming Wonder Woman or Superman. Many single parents juggling the demands of job and family have little idea what is in store for them when they marry someone else who has children. Once the wedding is over, reality hits home. Struggling to cope as spouse, parent, and stepparent, many people find themselves hungering to have their efforts recognized.

Stepparents seek recognition from their stepchildren. Even the most enlightened stepparent, knowing better than to expect instant love or gratitude from stepchildren, still wants to be appreciated. Many stepparents feel taken for granted, used. This feeling of being exploited becomes aggravated when children, who are simply trying to be loyal to their biological parent, make criticisms or comparisons like "Dad puts *lots* more butter on the popcorn" or "I like the way Mom reads that story better."

Stepparents want recognition from their stepchildren's absent parent. Most stepmothers want to have their parenting efforts acknowledged in some way by their stepchildren's mother; most stepfathers want this from the father. In either case, of course, this is the source from which they are least likely to get recognition. Thus, a standoff: the stepparent resents the same-sex biological parent for not appreciating all she or he is doing for this person's children; the biological parent resents the stepparent, seeing any parenting efforts as attempts to take his or her place.

A stepparent needs a spouse's emotional support. Stepparents who give a great deal of time and energy to caring for and supporting their spouse's children need to feel that they are appreciated and have their efforts validated. While a lack of recognition generally results in deep dissatisfaction, stepparents can take steps to improve the situation. They can begin by acknowledging that, especially at first, expecting recognition and gratitude is unrealistic. Then, they can begin to ask for what they need in this realm, especially from their spouse. Many people feel uncomfortable asking to have their efforts noticed. With practice, this discomfort lessens. Stepparents can also learn to give themselves pats on the back for their efforts and successes.

Stepparents can learn to give themselves pats on the back for their efforts and successes.

Competition—Creator of Conflict

As more people vie for the family's limited resources—especially money and time—competition in the stepfamily grows. Resources are often translated as love; their shortage can create conflict.

A husband's responsibility to a former mate and children usually means fewer resources for the new family. He may continue to care for his ex-wife's needs because she cares for his children. This may be hard for his new spouse to understand or accept, and can result in competition between the stepparent and the absent parent.

Competition with the same-sex parent may be played out by pretending the former spouse doesn't exist or by trying to outdo that person. The prize in this competition is the children's affections.

Competition with the same-sex parent might be displayed by outdoing.

Stepparents also compete with stepchildren for the spouse's attention and affection. For example, a stepson who looks like his father is a constant reminder that his mother—his stepfather's new wife—once loved another man. This physical resemblance may heighten the competition; so may teenage stepchildren themselves.

In all families, girls compete with their mother for their father's attention; boys compete with their father for their mother's. This natural sparring is one way young people validate their emerging sexuality. While biological parents find this competition annoying, stepparents find it maddening.

Unresolved competition can prevent the formation of strong family bonds. It can also breed jealousy. When unresolved issues from former marriages filter into the stepfamily, competition and jealousy can reach all-time highs. Jealousy destroys relationships and, ultimately, can undo the stepfamily.

Too many stepfamilies deal with negative feelings by denying them.

Jealous of my wife's former husband? Never. Resentful of my spouse's child support? Heck no—I knew about it. Guilty because I don't love his children? Not me! Afraid our stepfamily's in trouble? Of course not—we're just having adjustment problems.

Although it is a common way of dealing with resentment, guilt, anger, and fear, denial is dangerous for stepfamilies. It only dulls the hurt—it cannot erase the feelings. Continued denial pushes the pain deeper, increases feelings of doubt and jealousy, and creates more and more conflict.

The responsibility for reducing competition and jealousy in the stepfamily lies with both marriage partners. If competition is a problem in your stepfamily, use the skills and guidelines introduced in Chapter 2 to begin working to defuse it.

Responsibility—Personal and Legal

In most stepfamilies, time, space, and money are all in short supply. How much time should stepparents spend with stepchildren? Each stepparent needs time alone with her or his own children too. While partners understand this, they'd both prefer to spend more time alone—just the two of them. If children live with this new family only part-time, what is the expectation when they come for the summer or across town for the weekend? To catch up on time with one's own children, can a parent plan a camping trip without spouse and stepchildren? Will they feel left out? If that idea creates resentment, how *can* the parent spend quality time with the biological children, so dearly loved and rarely seen?

Time issues need to be talked about so resentment doesn't fester. Discussing different kinds of love is important, too, so children and stepchildren understand the adult's need for special time alone with each of them. Otherwise they fear being left out.

Money is the resource everyone seems to be short of. Stepparents often feel overwhelmed by the great financial responsibility they have taken on. Many continue to assist their first families to some degree, and wonder how they can stretch the paycheck between two homes. It is difficult for stepparents to accept the financial realities without resentment, to clarify exactly what they feel responsible for.

Resentment is a tricky emotion: The stepparent, while understanding the situation, even recognizing the need to help support the stepchildren, still wishes circumstances were different and resents the reality. The fact that neither the biological family nor the stepfamily seems to appreciate the step-parent's efforts further fuels this resentment. The stepparent may soon begin to resent *all* the changes that have come about.

"Why must I help support another person's children? Where, in this sea of responsibilities, can I find a spot to be alone?"

What about inheritance? What is the responsibility of a stepparent in this area? Most stepparents believe their primary responsibility is to their current spouse and their biological children, regardless of living arrangements. In terms of child support, the law upholds this, and in most states in the United States stepparents are not responsible for the financial support of stepchildren.

But what happens to the children after the biological parent dies? Must a parent entrust his or her estate to a former mate? Any claims by the ex-spouse should have been settled by the divorce, so that person should have no legal rights to the estate. If a parent is uncomfortable giving a former mate access to the estate in order to care for the children, that parent can establish a trust fund from which monthly checks will be released. Whatever arrangements are made, parent and stepparent should discuss them so the new spouse does not feel that a partner's financial loyalty to biological children leaves the new spouse out.

With a stepparent's resources spread between two families, stepchildren might only receive money indirectly later, through the husband's or wife's— their parent's—estate. Should you wish to leave part of your estate to your stepchildren, your will must be precise and specific. Most states do not rec-ognize stepchildren as having legal rights, so stating "all my children" in your will as an attempt to include your stepchildren might leave your intent open to interpretation.

Because the law, with regard to the stepfamily, remains filled with inconsis-tencies, many people turn to adoption. Adoption offers the only way to create a legal connection between unrelated children and adults in the stepfamily. Stepfamily adoptions, however, need to be approached cautiously. Some stepparents say adoption is a symbol of their commitment. But this permanent legal change in status neither guarantees a sense of belonging nor tightens bonds. While it might seem that adoption will solve problems concerning future inheritance, last names, or access to medical and school records, it can in reality put in motion a set of deeper, more far-reaching problems.

First and foremost, adoption requires the legal severing of a child's crucial relationship with the biological parent. Often, adults initiate the adoption process not with the child's best interest in mind, but because of their own need to push the ex-spouse out of the picture. Of course, formal adoption cannot actually erase the physical and emotional ties between this parent and child. Further, should the remarried couple later divorce, the legal adoptive relationship between stepparent and stepchild will *not* end. Adoptive stepparents hold the same lifetime responsibilities for their adopted stepchildren that they do for biological offspring.

Social workers and legal professionals are often insensitive to these crucial concerns. Although most adoptive parents are screened and counseled before they take on this serious legal commitment, stepparents who adopt rarely go through the same intensive process. Authorities tend to assume that because the people involved have lived together as a family, adoption is the natural solution for everyone. More often than not, this is simply not the case. Instead, what is done with good intentions may trigger a series of complicated psychological processes, actually damaging a once-healthy stepparent-stepchild relationship.

Instant Love

Like a favorite book you read and reread, the rewards of living in a stepfamily grow with the passage of time.

Among a stepparent's greatest stumbling blocks lies the myth of "instant love." When the belief that you can immediately love and be loved by your stepchildren proves unfounded, you will be left with one feeling: guilt. As a stepparent, you can reduce guilt about not loving your stepchildren: you can give yourself permission not to love them. It's that simple. Often, the only person telling you that you must love them is yourself. If your spouse has asked this of you, it's time to sit down and talk about reality. Explain the positive things you feel about your stepchildren and your hope that the relationships will grow. Reassure your spouse that you accept them, respect them, and will be patient with them as they adjust to their reorganized family. But make it clear that you will not be burdened with the expectation of loving children before you even get to know them.

The instant love myth can also set another common trap: a stepparent might demand love and acceptance from the children and insist on family unity. Measuring expectations in terms of harmony at all costs, this stepparent might dictate activities and deny free choices to family members, even diverting them from preferred activities so they can all be together as "one happy bunch." On the surface, family unity appears to have been achieved; under the facade, family members feel angry at being forced to do things they don't want to do. Soon, to meet their own needs, they will rebel, and the picture-perfect stepfamily will confront crisis as the stepparent is forced to revise expectations.

Like all things of value, stepfamily relationships take a long time to build. But, like a favorite book you read and reread, the rewards of living in a stepfamily grow with the passage of time. Once your stepfamily begins to develop shared memories and a sense of family history, you may find yourself liking your

Family unity cannot be forced.

stepchildren, feeling a sense of pride in their accomplishments. And in many, many stepfamilies the liking evolves to loving. It really does.

Struggling with Sexuality

Sexuality in the stepfamily affects all family members. The home of a remarried couple is probably far more sexually charged than a first-family home. Teenagers, as they deal with their own emerging sexuality, are especially affected. Feeling sexual attraction toward family members is normal in all families, but biological bonds and the "incest taboo" usually prevent feelings from being acted upon. With no such factors at work, many stepfamily members suffer from increased tension as they struggle with these normal feelings. Embarrassment keeps them from talking about their discomfort, yet these undisclosed sexual issues can threaten the very existence of the stepfamily.

Sexuality conflicts can exist in traditional families too. But blurred boundaries and stronger feelings in the stepfamily are more likely to cause confusion and inappropriate behavior. Sexuality is especially apparent in stepfamilies for two reasons.

Chart 3B

THE "INSTANT LOVE" EXPECTATION—DOWNHILL SLIDE TO TROUBLE

The problem begins with the unrealistic expectation itself.

It doesn't take stepparents long to realize they're not meeting the expectation they've set for themselves.

As they come to terms with this realization, many stepparents begin to feel inadequate and insecure. Some feel very guilty.

As the instant love expectation continues along its destructive path, trouble brews between stepparents and stepchildren, leading to conflict for the couple.

In a further effort to erase guilt, many stepparents look for evidence that their partner doesn't love his or her own child.

When stepparents expect to love their stepchildren immediately, they set themselves up for disappointment and failure. This chart depicts the downhill course such an "instant love" expectation takes.

Guilt often leads to resentment.

Resentment might lead the stepparent to find fault with the child and perhaps pick on the child unfairly.

Treating a stepchild unfairly causes the stepparent to feel even guiltier than before.

In an attempt to ease this guilt, the stepparent might conclude that the stepchild is unlovable.

This nine-phase progression is adapted from a model developed by Carolyn McClenahan, a marriage and family therapist in Los Gatos, California.

The children live with newlyweds. In first families, many children don't really notice their parents' sexuality. But the remarried parents' new couple relationship makes it obvious that sexual intimacy is an important part of their lives. They may give each other lingering kisses, touch openly, or stay in the bedroom for long periods of time. Their children see them responding to one another with embraces and affection unwitnessed in their parents' marriage as it came apart.

Many young people are uncomfortable with this awareness. Some are angry and resentful; others, embarrassed. When adolescents say they are bothered by their parents being "mushy," they are expressing anxiety about their own sexuality.

Adults in stepfamilies walk a fine line. Their children need to see the tenderness they feel toward one another; the couple's display of affection provides a positive role model for children as they develop their own concept of a marriage relationship. Watching parent and stepparent be close also gives children a secure feeling. But, somehow, to help the children deal with confused feelings, the family's view of the sexual part of the relationship must be minimized. When children are present, couples need to take care to keep their touching nonsexual.

Boundaries are blurred. The second reason that sexuality issues may cause greater tension in the stepfamily is that children now live with people they have not grown up with. Teenage stepbrothers and stepsisters may previously have been schoolmates—were perhaps already attracted to one another. Although they are now called sister and brother, their feelings may suggest something else. With no incest taboo to control the feelings, some stepsiblings could become lovers.

Experiencing feelings is one thing; acting on them, another. In our society, an intimate relationship between family members is forbidden—indeed illegal. Those who become involved feel guilty, and as guilt and fear of being found out increase, behavior toward other family members changes. The entire family suffers.

Similar feelings may occur between stepparents and stepchildren, but research shows stepfathers struggle with it most.[4] Many biological fathers also deal with sexual feelings as their daughters begin to blossom into young women. These feelings are normal, and most men control them. Recent revelations about the prevalence of incest prove, however, that some do not. Incest is a tragic crime, severely damaging the victims and affecting everyone in the family. For stepfathers, dealing with sexual feelings toward teenage stepdaughters is often extremely difficult: stepfamilies are not protected by the normal incest taboo.

Simple carelessness can enhance these difficulties. After living with their biological families for a long time, teenagers may have gotten used to casual living; walking around the house in underwear or nightclothes feels natural. Teenage stepchildren need to be told that this state of undress is inappropri-

Teenagers' embarrassment often reflects anxiety about their own sexuality.

ate. While an edict to don clothes or a robe might embarrass some stepfamily members, the warning could prevent deeper problems in the future.

Intentional sexual behavior by stepchildren is more complex. As girls mature, many try out their charms on their fathers, dressing provocatively and flirting to get feedback. Boys often behave the same way with their mothers. Am I attractive? Will the boys (or girls) like me? This behavior reflects normal adolescent development. Some teenagers, too, may use their sexuality in retaliation.

Perhaps a young man, angry at his father over his parents' divorce and the daily absence of his biological mother, may begin to flirt with his stepmother. Or, his provocations might reflect a normal teenage competition with his father.

Stepparents are likely to feel both stimulated and scared by this seduction. A stepfather*, while flattered by his stepdaughter's attention, also feels terribly guilty about his sexual thoughts and begins to fear he might act on them. In

*Similar situations occur between stepmothers and stepsons, but less often.

Guidelines for Addressing Sexuality in the Stepfamily

• Talk honestly and openly about sex and comfort levels. Discuss fears and feelings that might arise. Talk about and decide as a family what is appropriate behavior and dress.

• Anticipate and prevent situations where inappropriate sexual contact can occur. Teenage stepbrothers and stepsisters should not be left alone together for long periods of time.

• Establish home dress codes. Scanty lingerie and revealing jockey shorts are improper attire.

• Establish specific bathroom and bedroom etiquette. It's proper to knock before entering someone's room. Doors should be closed when someone is dressing or undressing, open when opposite-sex visitors are present. Bathroom doors can be locked, or an "In Use" sign hung from a nail on the door.

• Become aware of intense relationships or crushes. Talk openly about the fact that such feelings are normal, so family members do not feel guilty; but also establish and clarify what is acceptable in your home. Discuss the difference between feelings and behavior.

• Tune in when a family member expresses discomfort. Don't brush the statement aside—it might be a plea for help. Encourage conversation.

• If you feel sexually attracted to your stepchild, recognize that your feelings are normal. There is no reason to feel guilty about feelings. Realize, though, that *acting on* feelings by beginning a physical relationship will cause grief and guilt, delay the child's social development, and destroy your marriage.

---

many stepfamilies where sexuality is left undiscussed, moving from fantasizing to acting on feelings *does* happen. A stepfather might rationalize his behavior by thinking, "She isn't really my daughter."

Even when actual physical involvement doesn't occur, the home atmosphere can become extremely uncomfortable when it is sexually charged. If the couple relationship is poor and those involved cannot talk about what is happening, feelings of guilt, shame, and fear might prompt both people to protect themselves. Often, in such a situation, the stepfather will retreat and become overly critical of his stepdaughter. But at this important time in her identity struggle, the teenager needs validation that she is not only okay but, indeed, attractive. She may try harder to gain her stepfather's attention; he in turn retreats further. Not understanding why her stepfather, once playful and affectionate, has suddenly turned against her, she may feel rejected, interpreting his behavior to mean that he finds her unattractive or unlovable.

Many families never talk about sexuality; some because they are unconscious of the feelings, others because of the incest taboo. They think it is wrong to feel the way they do, and so, embarrassed and ashamed, they keep their feelings secret. These families fail to understand the difference between feelings, fantasy, and behavior. Sadly, feelings may suddenly get out of control and lead to a regrettable situation.

If you feel comfortable talking about sexuality in your stepfamily, by all means do so. Everyone will be relieved. If you cannot discuss the topic openly, seek help from a family counselor, a clergymember, or another uninvolved, non-judgmental third party.

Discipline Dilemma

Learning to discipline children effectively, so vital to the success of the step-family, is a book in itself. It is important here, however, to look at what's different about disciplining other people's children and what approach to discipline works best for the stepfamily.

In the beginning stages of stepfamily life, it is recommended that new step-parents leave much of the task of disciplining children to the biological parent. Why?

• Children are used to their parent's discipline style, and continuity in this arena is important at a time when so many other changes are taking place.

• Children adjust more easily to a new parental figure in their lives when the adult is not seen as an authority figure. They are given time to learn to respect and trust the stepparent; only then will children respond to the stepparent's discipline.

• The couple gains time to merge their differences, find what works for them, and learn parenting skills together in a class.

There are exceptions to this general guideline:

1. When the stepparent is the only parent at home. When you, the step-parent, are left alone with your stepchildren and they misbehave, you should not hesitate to take action. For this to work, the biological parent must transfer authority to you in front of the children.

"When I'm not home, we've agreed that Mike will be in charge. If a problem comes up, or if you need permission to do something, he'll make the decision."

2. When a child's misbehavior is directed specifically toward the step-parent. Here it is the stepparent's responsibility to respond.

If a child makes a mess with her stepmother's makeup, the stepmother needs to take action since the child's behavior directly affects her. If the same child refuses to brush her teeth, however, it is more appropriate for the biological parent—in this case, her father—to deal with the situation.

The couple's first task in dealing with discipline, then, is to learn what children are accustomed to and set an atmosphere of trust and respect. Later, after bonds have developed between stepparents and their stepchildren and couples have discussed and agreed on an overall discipline approach, it's appropriate for this task to be shared between the biological parent and the stepparent.

Keep in mind that dealing effectively with discipline is hardly a problem unique to stepfamilies. Nearly all parents find it a difficult task. And although children will misbehave as part of their stepfamily adjustment, don't interpret every action in this light.

A 12-year-old stepchild who displays a lot of rebellious behavior may not be showing hidden hostility toward the stepparent. The child may just be acting like a typical preteen, testing his own sense of power and control.

Remarried couples who persevere through the stressful times and finally achieve stepfamily stability speak of a strong sense of pride.

It is important to avoid viewing children's misbehavior as a sign that your stepfamily is failing. Instead, regard it as a signal that, to strengthen your stepfamily, you and your partner need to learn an approach to discipline that encourages children to cooperate and take responsibility for their own actions.

There are many fine books and programs available to parents who want to develop positive discipline methods.[5] The benefits of taking a class over simply reading about effective discipline techniques are many. A group setting offers stepfamily couples a chance to step back, explore their discipline techniques, and make a joint plan in an atmosphere that's supportive and encouraging. The group leader and other participants can offer valuable feedback during the process. For stepparents, who feel so isolated in their challenging roles, this peer support is very important. Classes give parents and stepparents time to try techniques at home and then return and discuss what happened. This valuable process will help them refine their skills.

What's Special about Being a Stepparent?

After exploring the many challenges of being a stepparent, one may wonder why anyone would take on such a role. Special joys *do* come from stepparenting. For the most part, rewards are long-term. But, when they come, they are well worth the investment.

Often a difficult and seemingly thankless task, being a stepparent can push adults to test their limits and tolerances. The challenges you face as a stepparent will unleash emotions that might otherwise remain buried within you. This can be very painful. Yet in confronting the powerful feelings and working through them with your stepchild or spouse, surmounting the problems and savoring the successes, you cannot help but experience growth and feel good about yourself.

Remarried couples who persevere through the stressful times and finally achieve stepfamily stability speak of a strong sense of pride. As they worked through their problems, becoming closer as a couple, they earned respect from their children, who witnessed a strong role model for marriage.

Another reward you may receive is a possibility, not a promise: you may develop a special relationship with a stepchild you see to adulthood. We all love our own children and hope to have that love returned; but with a stepchild, you may have a very special experience. Facing anger and resentment in spite of your best efforts, you may nonetheless struggle forward. Ultimately, you may grow to care deeply about that child; further, the two of you may have developed a bond of love. This very special love will have been earned, not through biology, but through respect, effort, and endurance. It happens for many stepparents. We hope it happens for you, too.

The promise of growth, the possibility of expanding the circle of love: these are the rewards you and your spouse can work for together.

Notes

1. Carol Cassell, "The Role of Stepmothers: A Comparative Study of Stepmothers With and Without Natural Children" (unpublished dissertation, University of New Mexico, 1981).

2. Emily B. Visher and John S. Visher, *Stepfamilies: A Guide to Working with Stepparents and Stepchildren* (New York: Brunner/Mazel, 1979). The same book, retitled *Stepfamilies: Myths and Realities,* is available in paperback from Citadel Press in Secaucus, New Jersey.

3. Paul Bohannan and Rosemary Erickson, "Stepping In," *Psychology Today* (January 1978).

4. Elizabeth Einstein, *The Stepfamily: Living, Loving, and Learning* (New York: Macmillan, 1982), pages 105-106.

5. We particularly recommend STEP—*Systematic Training for Effective Parenting,* and its companion program, STEP/Teen, by Don Dinkmeyer and Gary D. McKay; or *Active Parenting* by Michael H. Popkin. All are available from American Guidance Service, Circle Pines, MN 55014-1796. STEP parent-discussion groups are run regularly in community and church education programs throughout the United States, Canada, and Australia. The handbooks for either of the STEP programs are available in bookstores. For quick help on specific issues, try one of the books from Linda Albert's *Coping with Kids* series, also available in bookstores and from AGS.

References

Bernard, Jessie. *Remarriage.* New York: Russell and Russell, 1956.

Bustanoby, Andre. *The Ready-Made Family.* Grand Rapids, Mich.: Zondervan Publishing, 1982.

Capaldi, Fredrick, and Barbara McRae. *Stepfamilies: A Cooperative Responsibility.* New York: Newpoints/Vision, 1979.

Craven, Linda. *Stepfamilies: New Patterns of Harmony.* New York: Julian Messner, 1982.

Einstein, Elizabeth. *The Stepfamily: Living, Loving, and Learning.* New York: Macmillan, 1982; Boston: Shambhala, 1985.

Furstenberg, Frank, Jr., and Graham Spanier. *Recycling the Family: Remarriage after Divorce.* Beverly Hills: Sage Publications, 1984.

Sager, Clifford J. *Treating the Remarried Family.* New York: Brunner/Mazel, 1983.

Visher, Emily B., and John S. Visher. *Stepfamilies: Myths and Realities.* Secaucus, N.J.: Citadel Press, 1979.

Questions for Review

1. Of all the characteristics of an effective stepparent that have been discussed, which do you feel is the most important? Why? _____

_____

_____

2. What role do you play or hope to play in your stepchildren's life? How did you decide? Do you think the children agree about what role they want you to play? Explain why you feel as you do. _____

_____

_____

3. Why might it be important for stepparents to choose their role rather than slip into it? _____

_____

_____

4. In which kind of stepfamily configuration do you live? What is your greatest stumbling block and why? What could help you transform that stumbling block to a success? _____

_____

_____

5. If you are both a parent and a stepparent, how do you manage to balance your time between your stepchildren and your biological children? _____

_____

_____

6. Have you had, or can you imagine having, a conversation with the nonresidential parent about your stepchildren? What do you want to share? What do you want to know? What are your fears? _____

_____

_____

7. Can you identify your most important need as a stepparent? Your partner's?

_____

_____

8. What was your most unrealistic expectation about becoming a stepparent? How did you, or might you, resolve it? _____

_____

_____

9. Have you and your spouse clarified the levels of responsibility you have toward your stepchildren? Where do you still feel unclear? _____

_____

_____

10. What are some problems that adoption of stepchildren in your family might cause? _____

_____

_____

11. How do you deal with sexuality issues in your stepfamily? If you've avoided discussion of sexuality, is there a reason? Where can you begin? ____

_____

_____

12. Why is it important for the biological parent to assume the role of disciplinarian with her or his own children rather than let the stepparent take over immediately? _____

_____

_____

Challenge to Conquer

Two weeks ago, Claire's 13-year-old stepdaughter Fé had her girlfriend stay overnight. As they watched TV with the girls, Claire and her husband Brad were feeling especially romantic. They began hugging and kissing and soon got up to leave. The couple headed for the bedroom, giggling, seemingly oblivious to the teenagers or anyone else in the home. Whispering intimately, they closed the door. Later, Fé knocked tentatively on the bedroom door to ask about plans for the next day. "Go away," Brad shouted. When the girl persisted, Claire called, "Not *now*, Fé."

Since then, Fé will hardly speak to Claire or Brad. She's also stopped having her best friend over, saying she prefers to go to her friend's house instead.

1. What might Fé be thinking and feeling? Why has she withdrawn from the family? _____

_____

_____

2. How might Claire and Brad be feeling about Fé's behavior? _____

_____

_____

3. How can Brad and Claire empathize with Fé? What is she experiencing? What feelings did her parent and stepparent's behavior arouse in her? _____

_____

_____

Activity for the Week

Discipline is a big issue for stepfamilies. This week, you and your mate can each write down answers to the three questions that follow. Then get together to compare responses and begin discussing a shared discipline approach.

1. Here are a number of ways parents discipline their children. Check which techniques you now use:

yelling_____ nagging_____ reminding_____ giving choices_____ punishing_____ I-messages_____ negotiating_____ spanking_____ rewarding_____ family meetings_____ requesting_____ establishing limits_____ ignoring_____ consequences_____ setting up automatic rules and routines_____ bribing_____ involving_____ threatening_____ encouraging_____ resolving conflicts_____ using incentives_____

2. Which techniques are you now using that you'd like to stop? _____

_____

_____

3. Which techniques would you like to learn more about? _____

_____

_____

Compare your list with your mate's. Are they the same or different? Discuss steps you can take to begin to develop common discipline strategies.

Points to Ponder

- Effective stepparents
  - are able to empathize.
  - are not defensive.
  - avoid being judgmental.
  - show acceptance.
  - are open to change.
  - have a strong sense of personal identity.
  - believe in children's abilities and allow them to be responsible for themselves.

- Stepparents can play one or more roles in stepchildren's lives: friend, confidant, another parent figure, mentor, role model. Couples need to discuss and agree about what role the stepparent will take.

- Remarried noncustodial parents with stepchildren often cope with guilt about rearing someone else's children rather than their own.

- Stepparents need validation and support from friends and family. Mostly, they need it from their spouse.

- Unchecked competition creates jealousy among stepfamily members that can hinder building bonds.

- The law cannot legislate love. Adoption is not a cure-all for the stepfamily.

- The idea of instant love between stepfamily members is absurd. Refuse to believe this notion, giving yourself permission not to love your stepchildren.

- Sexuality issues must be discussed in the stepfamily. Not doing so can lead to serious consequences.

- At the start, in stepfamilies, it is most effective when biological parents discipline their own children.

Understanding My Stepfamily

1. Giving thanks. Think about some of the ways you appreciate your partner for helping you rear your children. A note of thanks for "being aboard" or a simple statement like "Khanh, I appreciate your willingness to help Eric with the model for the Scouts' derby. I hope it was fun for you, too," will make a big difference to your partner. Take a moment to list the things you appreciate in your spouse as a stepparent to your children.

_____

_____

_____

_____

_____

_____

2. The misguided and the effective stepparent. Complete the following:

Here's what I now do that is effective: _____

_____

Here's what I now do that is misguided: _____

_____

Here's what I plan to change or do differently: _____

_____

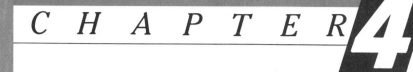

CHAPTER 4

The Stepchild's Dilemmas

L ast night I asked my almost seven-year-old daughter what she wanted for her birthday. She hesitated for a minute, casting her stepfather, Mitch, an apologetic glance. Then she said, 'I want you and Daddy to get married to each other again.' 'Honey,' I told her, 'you know that can't happen . . . What else do you want?' This time her reply was quick and cheerful: 'To go camping with you and Mitch. Will you take me?'"

Childhood is a small part of one's life, yet what happens then influences the rest. Much has already transpired in the lives of stepchildren, causing them sadness and loss. Children *do* adapt to such traumatic losses. Their adjustment depends on how well they are helped through the mourning process. When you remarried, your children's mourning may have been incomplete. It is natural for them to carry some scars and confused memories into the stepfamily. In fact, when they become stepchildren, anxiety over their loss may actually intensify. Old fears resurface, new ones appear, and stepchildren feel surrounded with uncertainty. As you start your stepfamily with enthusiasm and high hopes, your children may respond with confusion and anger.

The questions children of loss rarely verbalize but carry heavy in their hearts are rooted in fears. "Where do I belong? Will I still see my dad?" "If I learn to like this new person, will Mommy be upset?" While your remarriage can ultimately provide a new stability for your children, it will not immediately calm their fears. It will take time to lower their anxiety and rebuild their trust.

This chapter focuses on the children in your stepfamily and the dilemmas they face as they adjust to stepfamily living. Exploring some of your children's specific interrelationships will help you see life in the stepfamily from their perspective. As you learn what to expect, you can begin to understand some of the reasons behind your children's actions. You will be in a better position to respond in ways that help your children and your entire stepfamily.

Emotional Dilemmas— Mourning and Healing

Whether a first marriage ends through death or divorce, part of the adults' healing process includes getting rid of anger and learning to trust again. Children, too, need to heal. Children in remarriages often harbor many leftover negative feelings: anger, sadness, guilt, fear, and resentment.

Anger. Your children had no choice in the matter of the divorce or death. Their response to this lack of control in their lives may be anger toward either parent, but particularly toward the biological parent with whom they live daily. They may have lost their sense of security and regular contact with friends and relatives. They may blame the custodial parent for having to move. Teenagers especially want to feel they have choice and control in their lives.

Learning to trust again is difficult for children. They thought they could always count on their family; when the family ended, they were dramatically let down. Such a loss may shatter their trust in adults, including their own parent, for some time.

Guilt. Guilt, the inability to forgive oneself, is another emotion your children struggle with. While guilt is common to all stepfamily members, in children it is usually repressed and hard to detect. Many children blame themselves for their parents' break-up, sometimes even for the death of a parent. Such thoughts bring on feelings of unworthiness that can cause some children to set themselves up for failure. Retreating from friends and activities may be some children's way of making up for what they believe they did wrong. Creating displeasure with parents adds yet another deprivation that helps children relieve their imagined guilt.

Although parents may explain the death or divorce, if the explanation is unclear or hostile, children may create their own reasons for what happened. These versions may be irrational and far from the truth; unenlightened, children live out their misperceptions in their stepfamilies and, later, in relationships as adults.

To help them understand, adults need to give children straightforward but nonjudgmental answers. Children are far better off living with the truth than complicating their lives with incorrect assumptions that must one day be cleared up. Most questions will concern what happened with the other parent.

"Why did my parent leave? Why did our family end?"

Although it may upset you to rehash your divorce, remember that your children's identity comes from *both* parents. When one is missing, an important part of that child is missing too. Speak honestly but discreetly as you fill in the gaps. Remember, no matter how you feel about a former spouse, your child has an innate love for that person. It's a mistake to put down the ex-spouse. When this is done, some children—to reconcile what they've been told with what they need to hear—will fantasize about the other parent. These fantasies can rival fairy tales. It's also a mistake to go to the other extreme, idealizing the missing parent. This can cause children to become caught up in loyalty conflicts and inhibit their relationships with stepparents.

The best gift you can give your children is the permission to have a relationship with their other parent without your interference. The situation may not be ideal, it may not be what you wish for your children; yet it allows children to learn more about another part of themselves and sidestep some of the loyalty dilemmas they might otherwise face. And, by maintaining positive ties with both parents, children gradually develop their own sense of justice and rid themselves of guilt.

Fear. Stepchildren fear losing another family. After all, they've been through that already. Any increasing conflict levels in your home, possibly even threats of divorce, may raise those fears again.

Often, juggling a job, family, and new spouse leaves a parent little time for children. When this happens, children may begin to wonder if their parent still loves them. They may cling to their biological parent and avoid developing closeness with the new stepparent. Since trust is already low and there is no guarantee the adults can make this marriage work, children will be slow to form bonds.

The best gift you can give your children is the permission to have a relationship with their other parent without your interference.

Your children may fear a shift or loss in the relationship with you and feel resentful about your remarrying. This is especially likely if they are teenagers, already undergoing many changes in their own lives, or if you stayed single for a long time. Having lived together in a close, successful single-parent family, you and your children may have developed a special closeness. Now, the children may not want to share time and space with another adult. Above all, they resent having to share you.

With their familiar family structure gone, children face the unknown. One way they may show their fear and confusion is through misbehavior. This is normal. Very young children might cling, wet the bed, or withdraw. Sudden mood swings are common; so are tantrums and drops in school grades. Teenagers might respond by turning to sex or drugs. Until children find their place in the family and feel your remarriage is secure, they may test you—over and over.

Your decision to remarry may have been a wise one for all concerned. Released from an unfulfilling marriage or a life of loneliness, you began again, probably becoming a better parent as you were able to provide your children with a happier family atmosphere. It would be a mistake, though, to expect your children to feel as happy as you do about your remarriage; this would be a sure way to set yourself up for disappointment! Yet, although experiencing death or divorce and remarriage is difficult, it can teach children how to adapt to changes and demands made upon them. As they learn to get along with people outside their immediate family, they develop flexibil-

Children may test you—sometimes to the limit.

ity. New role models with new, perhaps very different, values can teach your children a lot. As they come to terms with two sets of rules about life, your children learn to make choices. Someday, after children work through their feelings, they may say, "Thanks for the fresh start."

Guidelines for Helping Children
Through the Healing Process

• Be aware of all the changes in children's lives over which they had no control and be sensitive to their feelings.

• Ease into the newness of the stepfamily, realizing that children's uncertainty is normal.

• Be patient and answer children's questions honestly and carefully.

• Accept grief and loss as part of life and encourage children to face the reality of these losses. Empathize, rather than sympathize, with them. Help them to express their anger and sadness.

• Encourage children's relationship with their other biological parent. Never undermine that relationship.

• Reach out with assurance of love and show continued caring. Nurture children with extra hugs, "I love yous," and time spent together. (Don't, however, confuse nurturing with pitying, pampering, or overprotecting.)

• Confront misbehavior and take corrective steps. Do not make excuses for children's inappropriate actions.

Coping with a New Stepparent

If most stepkids had their way, they would not have stepparents: they'd rather have both biological parents living together. This wish has little to do with the stepparents themselves and a lot to do with the children's losses. But since a stepparent is a reality, children must figure out where to fit this person into their complicated lives.

The decisions begin with names—what children should call the stepparent. The terms *mom* and *dad* describe biological relationships and have strong emotional connotations; forcing children to use these words in reference to stepparents creates discomfort. Very young children might eagerly call stepparents Mommy or Daddy; older children may prefer to use first names. Some children use different parental names for stepparents, such as Pop or Mama Jane. Stepparents' first names may evolve into Dad or Mom, when and if children develop an emotional bond with the stepparent. The final word about naming and introductions rests with how comfortable children are with the names; stepparents should feel content with them, too.

Choosing names is only the beginning. On a deeper level, children must ask themselves, "What can this stepparent be for me?" Should the new stepparent be immature emotionally, demanding a great deal of the biological parent's time and attention, he or she will become an intruder in children's eyes. First they lost daily contact with one parent; now the other is unavailable. Their

It's important to settle on a name agreeable to all.

resentment can lead to power plays and triangles that threaten the stability of the stepfamily.

The biological parent, by encouraging the children to begin building a relationship with the new spouse, can help keep resentment at bay. The parent can be sure to preserve her or his own relationship with the children by having special time together, apart from activities with the entire stepfamily.

Children form ideas about the role they want their stepparent to play in their lives after assessing many things—the kind of person the stepparent is, hobbies and interests the person pursues, age, whether the stepparent has children. They will take into account their own needs, too, and how they believe this new adult can help meet them. How children fit the stepparent into their lives will also depend on their own age and development. The relationship they have with their own parents will affect their decision, too.

Such choices are rarely made on a conscious level. But, consciously or unconsciously, children will form expectations about this new relationship. They may cast the stepparent in one or more of the roles discussed in Chapter 3: friend, confidant, parent figure, mentor, role model. It's important for parent and stepparent to be aware of each child's expectations and to consider how appropriate they are. What children think they want may not always be in their best interests.

Guidelines for Helping Children Adjust to a Stepparent

• Recognize the importance of the other biological parent and respect children's right and need to love that parent. Support the time they spend with their other family and invite that parent and other family members to milestone ceremonies—recitals, play-offs, graduations. At such events, focus only on the children and put aside unfinished emotional business between adults present.

• Never speak negatively of the other parent in front of the children; control any resentment you may feel.

• As a stepparent, acknowledge the strong bond between your new spouse and his or her children. So children won't feel left out, avoid monopolizing your mate's time.

• Plan "alone time" with your stepchildren so you can get to know one another better. *Invite* them to do things with you—don't pressure them or make demands.

• Understand that family life cannot always be happy. When conflict arises, it doesn't mean that your family is failing or that your stepchildren hate you.

• Don't expect "instant love": allow time for relationships to develop. Concentrate on learning to accept, respect, and like your stepchildren.

• Reject fairy-tale myths and unrealistic media portrayals of stepfamilies. Forgive yourself for being imperfect. Realize that you learn when you make mistakes. So does your spouse, and so do the children!

Coping with Differences

Picture your values and beliefs, all the information you impart to your children to help them make their way in the world, as a pair of prescription eyeglasses that you give them. Although some children may refuse to wear them, rejecting their parents' values, most tend to or will generally come to view the world through these or similar lenses.

Your children learned to make judgments and evaluations based on what you taught them. Your beliefs and behavior provided their frame of reference. When people responded in certain ways to their behavior, life became somewhat predictable; that predictability meant a certain security.

Enter a new stepparent with another set of lenses. Children must now learn to use two separate, sometimes very different, sets of lenses to view the world. Asked to adapt to these new "eyeglasses," children may have a fuzzy, if not downright chaotic, view of life; they may respond with erratic behavior.

This "double vision" gets more complicated. As stepchildren spend time at Mom's home and Dad's, they cope with different beliefs and behavior in two households. First they must deal with stepparents and stepsiblings in the home where they live; then they must ease into yet another way of doing things in the home of the noncustodial parent, who may also have remarried.

Adjusting may cause difficulties, but those difficulties aren't insurmountable. Remember, children are already accustomed to making a variety of adjustments. They adjust daily to different teachers, different sitters, the changing behavior of family and friends. The key is for adults to acknowledge, without judging, the differences children are experiencing and then to state expectations: "Yes, it *is* different between Daddy's home and Mommy's. Here, we do it this way."

Gradually, these adjustments can be made. Adults who understand the specific differences children face will be better able to help ease things along.

Children face differences <u>at home</u>. Day-to-day living rooted in two separate histories will call for changes. When two sets of people with different backgrounds try to live with one another, routine matters such as mealtimes, chores, personal habits and hygiene can come under scrutiny. People have individual ways of doing things, but family members who grew up together will be more likely to do things similarly.

Do you eat chicken with your fingers? How do you hold your fork? Are pancakes large and thin, or silver-dollar-size? Do you fold towels into thirds and stack them, hems out? Do you towel-dry dishes, or let them dry in a dish drainer?

In first families everyone knows what is expected and no one thinks much about these everyday routines: things are simply done a certain way. To get used to *new* ways, family members need time. Too much change too quickly upsets everyone. Problems begin when stepparents try to change things, discounting the way someone else has always done them. Some family members may feel attacked.

It's critical for stepfamilies to talk about the specifics of daily routines in former families or in the other parent's home. Discuss mealtimes, dress codes, school, homework, morning and bedtime schedules—rules, responsibilities, and routines. Use such discussions for discovery, not for deciding which way is right. Avoid criticism or ridicule of someone else's way. Where choices are necessary, make compromises.* Above all, remember: neither approach to a task is *right* or *wrong;* each is simply a different way of doing things.

Children face differences <u>between homes</u>. As stepchildren move between two homes, they must deal with even more differences. Children may be used to the way their biological parent in the other home has been doing things, but when that parent remarries, more differences complicate their

---

*A companion publication to this book, *The Encouragement Packet: At-Home Activities for Strengthening Your Stepfamily,* includes many activities to help you introduce and guide these discussions. *The Encouragement Packet* is available from American Guidance Service, Circle Pines, Minnesota 55014-1796.

Differences in rules and routines will take some getting used to.

lives. When caught between the two families, children may have a strong need to protect the parent with whom they live. They may resort to criticism of the stepparent. On the other hand, if children begin to develop a friendship with the stepparent, biological parents may feel threatened and talk negatively about that adult.

When adults keep in mind that their children are family members of two separate households, the moves between two homes become a little easier for all concerned. Family boundaries that are open and flexible work best. While basic decisions and authority lines need to come from the home in which children live most of the time, kids need to know they are loved by both parents and accepted in both homes.

Many benefits exist in stepfamily living. In fact, stepfamily members often find it ironic: differences that once caused problems become possibilities they never thought of before. Most also say that, after an adjustment period, they changed, becoming more adaptable. Experts find this to be especially true of children—*if* the children are not burdened by their parents' unresolved problems. Change, when met without resistance or ridicule from adults, can enrich the lives of stepchildren. Learning to view the world through several different lenses gives them a head start on getting along with many kinds of people in their lives.

Having a Noncustodial Parent

It is rare for a noncustodial parent to be unimportant to a stepchild. Once a parent, always a parent; divorce does not diminish that reality. Dead or alive, parents are a shaping factor in our lives. When a parent has died, memories of that person linger in the child's mind forever; very young stepchildren even fantasize that their dead parent might return. If divorce ended the marriage, the other parent is the person with whom the children and you or your spouse will continue to interact.

You know that stepfamily stability hinges on the quality of your couple relationship. It is also affected by the degree to which the parent without custody accepts, and is accepted by, your stepfamily. Kids have a right to relationships with both their parents. Since adults divorce each other but not their children, the noncustodial parent—a symbol of the first marriage—is a vital connection in the network of stepfamily relationships.

Your children's visits with their other parent may be irregular; they may not represent the quality parent-child relationship you would like. But your children and stepchildren are better off for having that contact with their other parent. While it may seem that day-to-day stepfamily living could be easier without continued contact, closing off any relationship with the noncustodial parent ultimately creates more problems for the children.

The absent parent can be friend or foe to you and your stepfamily. If adult relationships are charged with unresolved hostility, this link between two families can create problems for stepchildren. Positive relationships, on the other hand, make the connection a source of strength that can help build and eventually stabilize the stepfamily.

Children adjust to seeing their other parent infrequently as long as, in some way, they are shown they are loved.

The secrets to being a successful part-time parent are consistency and continuity. Consistency means having an agreement to be firm but fair, faithful to the established rules and limits. Continuity means keeping up an ongoing relationship by spending recurring meaningful time with the children. After a divorce, many biological parents play a diminished role in their children's lives. A person in this position isn't in any way less a parent, but not being involved daily makes it difficult to function like one. It takes hard work to cope with guilt about not seeing one's children often; and it takes persistence to maintain a strong parent-child relationship in spite of time and distance constraints. Children adjust to seeing their other parent infrequently as long as, in some way, they are shown they are loved.

Love vs. "Stuff"

Some noncustodial parents feel so guilty about their diminished role that they try to make up for it during visits. Every stepfamily knows about the overindulgent absentee parent. But, more than *presents,* children need *presence* from this parent they so rarely see. Although gifts are welcome expressions of caring, *time* with their other parent is what children need and seek. Most children prefer getting time and caring from their parents to getting "stuff." This is especially true for children of divorce who need to know, above all, that they are loved.

Quality time is shared time: it need not mean a special event or high cost. Amusement parks and movies can be fun, but a steady diet of such activities sets up a poor long-term relationship with the noncustodial parent. Fixing a car, playing a board game, taking a hike, or even watching television together all provide chances for parents and children to share—without making elaborate plans or spending lots of money. There are also many creative and inexpensive ways for absentee parents to remain an active part of their children's lives. Phone calls, tapes, letters, and postcards all remind stepchildren that, although they cannot be together, their other parent often thinks of them. A clever book, *101 Ways to Be a Long-Distance Super-Dad* (Blossom Valley Press, Mountain View, California 94040), shows absentee mothers and fathers creative ways they can maintain relationships with their children—even from three thousand miles away.

Guidelines for Helping Children Move Between Homes

• Let the other parent and your children and stepchildren know they can count on you for support.

• Be willing to talk over any problems that arise during the transition between homes. If you're still angry at your former spouse and cannot communicate directly, try dealing with your ex-mate's partner about the children's transitions.

• Visits to the other parent may be irregular, but when they are planned, help the children prepare emotionally. They need to know they'll be missed, but since they may already be anxious about going, avoid adding more stress by bringing up complaints about chores or messy rooms right before they leave.

• Simplify and neutralize transitions. Perhaps the other parent could pick the children up from school or the ballpark—some neutral spot. When children return home, avoid greeting them at the door; allow them a few minutes alone in their room to adjust. Don't give them the third degree.

• Be firm but flexible in your dealings with the other parent. Cooperation reduces tension.

• Unless the children are teenagers, adults should make the visiting arrangements among themselves, so children are not caught in the middle.

• Be flexible. As children grow, their needs change. Their time becomes filled with friends and activities. Help them tell their other parent why they don't want to come every weekend, even though the custody agreement decrees it. If you are the noncustodial parent, try to understand and accept children's changing needs.

• With younger children, suggest taking a toy or game to break the ice in the other home.

• Never use the children as money messengers, and don't send lists of things you want the other parent to do or buy.

• Allow children to talk about their time with their other parent if they wish, but don't pry. Just listen.

Sometimes, the biological parent without custody is seen as an unfit parent. Should children be allowed time with such a person? Unfortunately, situations do exist where parents need to protect their children from abusive parents or dangerous living arrangements. But many times a noncustodial parent is labeled unfit either because of value differences or as a reflection of anger by the former spouse. As a custodial parent, it is important to determine whether your former mate is truly unfit and would endanger your child, or whether you are simply projecting unresolved hostility. Perhaps your former spouse is not the ideal parent, but is this person truly dangerous or a poor role model for your children? Or do you still harbor intense hostility for being wronged?

A competition often exists between divorced adults. The contest's prize: the children's love and affection. Some kids use this explosive situation to get what they want from their parents. If children cannot have what they really want—their family intact and the assurance that they are loved—they try for "stuff." Since parents need to be loved, too, they often say *yes* when *no* is most appropriate. By pitting parent against parent, children win prizes and privileges, but these make for a hollow victory. Until divorced parents cooperate rather than compete, their children may continue to maneuver them in this way.

Besides going after material possessions, children might use the "I'm gonna go live with Dad (Mom)" threat to get their way. By caving in to this threat, adults are permitting children to avoid facing conflict at home. If they are allowed to flee to the other home, children learn only to run from difficulties and avoid responsibility.

Schools Can Help or Hinder

Another crucial adjustment and communication link can be provided by the school. School can be a stabilizing force for children during a parent's divorce and remarriage—if teachers and parents work together. When educators are aware of stepfamily dynamics and the individual family's special needs, schools can respond by serving as partners in children's growth and adjustment.

But this partnership, like so many others, may suffer from an information gap. When communication between school and stepfamily is unclear or nonexistent—when educators don't know a family is reorganized and families don't know what to do to get the school's help—children's development can be hindered.

Today, nearly one-fifth of the children in American classrooms under the age of 18 are involved in some sort of step-relationship.[1] That figure is likely to grow, because, if current trends continue, nearly half of all American children born during the 1970s will experience divorce and most will become stepchildren. Yet, as common as remarriage is, a school-stepfamily information gap often still exists.

Chart 4A

DON'T TAKE IT PERSONALLY

All children in all families have some basic needs that must be fulfilled: They need a sense of security and belonging. They need to feel important and significant as persons. Children in stepfamilies, who have experienced many losses and changes, often find it difficult to get these needs met. Inwardly fearful, anxious, or confused, they may react outwardly with behavior that baffles and upsets stepparents.

In turn, stepparents often assume responsibility for stepchildren's actions. "What did I do?" many ask. Usually, this defensive reaction just makes things worse. It's important to realize that stepchildren's behavior might stem from any number of sources having nothing to do with the stepparent. Adults who understand this can reduce their own negative reactions.

Do your stepkids ever behave like the children on this chart? If so, don't take it personally!

> I DON'T WANNA HEAR YOUR DUMB OLD STORY— GO READ TO SOMEBODY ELSE !

A stepchild with whom you've had an excellent relationship may suddenly rebel and reject you. You didn't do anything. At some point, children have to cope with the reality that their parents are not going to get back together. Children coming to terms with this often rebel.

> WILL MOMMY MIND THAT I HAD FUN WITH DADDY'S NEW WIFE?

Children who are not given clear, direct permission from biological parents to develop warm relationships with stepparents often feel caught in loyalty conflicts.

Stepsiblings may feel jealous or resentful when they have to share their biological parent's time and attention. If they have lived with a single parent for a long time, the adjustment is especially difficult.

Gaining a stepchild's trust takes time and patience. Stepchildren fear another loss: they have no assurance that their new stepparent will not leave them just as their other parent did.

Very young children may fear that because one parent has gone, their other parent will leave as well. This is especially true if a parent has died or abandoned a child. Some children even give up friends and play activities in order to cling to the biological parent. Disconcerting as this may be to stepparents, it is a phase many children must pass through as they relinquish one parent and rebuild trust in the other.

When school policies close out noncustodial parents or stepparents, the schools can pose a threat to parent-child relationships. Forcing children to choose parent over stepparent or parent over parent creates divided loyalties.

How is a child to distribute the two tickets allotted for the school play? Who gets invited? Who doesn't? When teachers limit the number of presents made on Mother's Day or Father's Day, how is the child to choose whether to give the gift to the parent or the stepparent?

Since language both reflects and determines beliefs, the words teachers use to refer to divorced and remarried families will affect their students. Uninformed teachers can use language that sabotages efforts being made at home.

One child came home from school frightened, insisting his parent come outside and walk all around their house with him. He was looking for cracks because his teacher had said he came from a "broken home."

Children know most broken things don't work! Many single-parent families and stepfamilies, however, *do* work—very well. When children hear expressions like "broken home," "shattered family," "natural parent," or "failed marriage" they form a negative image of their own or their classmates' families.

Many textbooks continue to portray only the never-divorced family. Unable to identify with the families in their schoolbooks, children who live in nontraditional families may feel left out. They may wonder if something is wrong with their kind of family.

If educators are insensitive to stepfamily dynamics, school conferences can create further difficulties. A teacher who feels uncomfortable with divorced or remarried parents may inadvertently shift the focus of the meeting from the children's progress to coping with the intrusive feelings.

School counselors who understand a student's family configuration can better help that child. Unfortunately, many never ask about the family; some even consider it irrelevant to the child's school life. But emotions have a great effect on a child's performance in school. How can children learn while their heads and hearts are in turmoil? As they worry about how they will fit in with all these new people, when and if they will see their grandparents, whether their new stepparent will stay, children's concentration dwindles and their studies suffer.

Closing the Gap

The gap between schools and stepfamilies serves only to intensify confusion for everyone in the stepfamily. Closing the gap begins with you. While schools have a responsibility to your stepfamily, they need your cooperation. It's up to you to let your child's teachers know about the changed status of your family and to work with schools to normalize within the classroom the image of stepfamilies.

It's up to you to let your child's teachers know about the changed status of your family and to work with schools to normalize within the classroom the image of stepfamilies.

Contact might be through a formal letter or a telephone call. If this can be done before the remarriage, all the better. When teachers have a clue to what's happening at home, they can approach classroom difficulties with knowledge and understanding; they can talk with children to help lessen fears.

Clarify relationships and lines of responsibility. Let the school know exactly who has the right to interact with your child. Who can take the children from school? Your ex-spouse remains a parent, and you will want to work with the schools so that she or he is not left out of your child's life. Administrators who misinterpret the Buckley Amendment[2] or who are not sensitive to stepfamily dynamics might view the noncustodial parent as a nonparent.

Ask teachers to integrate words like *stepparent, stepfather,* and *stepmother* into classroom conversations. Encourage schools to purchase textbooks and library books portraying a variety of family units and lifestyles and to let publishers know of this need. Talk with your children about their relationship with the school to learn how they think stepfamilies could be better served. Tell them to speak out if they hear negative language about stepfamilies and to let you know if they fail to get the support they deserve from a counselor.

Living with Stepsiblings

Stepsibling arithmetic seems simple enough: addition. With more children, there's more interaction, more rivalry and competition, more fighting—and more fun. But, for a while, it mostly seems like more fighting!

Most siblings fight. Like adults, they fight to get what they want and to get their needs met. When sisters and brothers raise the roof, sibling rivalry can drive most parents crazy. When children from two or more families come together, this rivalry often intensifies. Stepsiblings fight over the same things biological brothers and sisters do—parental favoritism, family position, space, time, and possessions. Mostly, they fight about having to share a parent. Learning to share a parent in a biological family is a tough enough task; learning to share a parent after experiencing loss and while trying to jockey for a place in the new family is doubly hard.

Stepsibling Rivalry

Competition is common to all families. Sibling rivalry begins when first-born children must learn to cope with the addition of a new sibling who threatens their role and position in the family. Until their parents can reassure them that there is enough love to go around, they may feel displaced or "dethroned." Older children who have a hard time sharing the limelight with the newcomer may display outright hostility. Troubles among stepbrothers and stepsisters, however, are more complicated than this.

Stepsiblings may resent one another. All fear the loss of time with their own parent whom they now have to share. They fear a loss of space and privacy and, in part, this fear is justified. Sharing space means adjustments; children have less space for their belongings and no way to decorate a place exclusively as their own, creating a personal identity. A loss of privacy means no place to be alone with friends. Worse, it means no place to be alone with oneself—to dream and plan.

When biological sisters and brothers fight, they share a loyalty that carries them through the troubles. Feeling loyal to their parents, their blood relationship, and their family, they know they must sooner or later resolve or accept their differences. Most eventually do. Stepsiblings feel no such kinship; many don't even feel they belong to the family. With both sets of children feeling this way, what incentive do they have to get along? As the children fight for their place in the new family constellation, sibling rivalry in stepfamilies can become extremely serious.

If only one partner brings children to the remarriage, sibling rivalry won't be *substantially* different from what it was before the remarriage. But in families with stepsiblings, adults need to encourage feelings of importance and belonging in all children and assure them that this new family is secure.

Guidelines to Help Support Stepsibling Relationships

• Help children accept the fact that things have changed for them. Help them come up with creative ways to make private space for themselves when they do have to share.

• Tell children that you expect them to live respectfully together.

• Model effective communication and problem-solving techniques so children see positive ways of coping with conflict.

• Teach children to say what they feel and avoid blame games. Help them express their feelings through I-messages: "I feel angry when someone uses my things without asking."

• Schedule a regular meeting time in which the whole family gets together to discuss routines, make plans, explore expectations, and air and iron out grievances. (See "Coming Together—The Stepfamily Meeting" later in this chapter.)

• Avoid interfering. As long as children aren't doing serious physical or emotional harm to one another, stepparents and parents will be wise to let the kids work out their problems among themselves, without parental interference. Above all, avoid being pulled into triangles. Children who work through their own problems end up being better friends.

• Remember that stepsibling affection cannot be forced. It develops slowly and naturally or not at all. Be patient as stepsiblings struggle to accept their new situation and move forward.

How? The couple can make it clear to children that this marriage is a serious, lifetime commitment. Children need to hear this kind of confirmation so they will neither worry nor harbor false hopes about the marriage ending. The couple can plan activities for the whole stepfamily that will give family members an opportunity to have fun together, get to know each other better, and solve conflicts creatively. By arranging shared chores or special times during which parents do something together with two stepsiblings who need to get along better, adults can encourage children to interact in a setting that is limited and defined.

Parents and stepparents should also help each child find private time and space for daydreaming, sorting out personal problems, and just being alone. Families come up with many ingenious ways of making private space for people. Creating a makeshift room divider out of a sheet or blanket can be a project children enjoy. If space is very limited, children can have their own cupboard or drawer. In homes with tight bedroom space, each child can have his or her own bulletin board or corner of the room to decorate. Left to their own devices, some children will improvise to find space they feel they need.

If a child takes her toys off to the laundry room or gravitates to a dusty corner of the basement to do homework, adults can be sensitive and alert to the child's efforts to find some privacy. They can support the child's right to this time alone and even help arrange seating or lighting.

Birth Order Reshuffled

One very significant long-term effect in many remarriages is a shift in family birth order. A major force affecting the lives of children is the position they were born into in the family. First child? Last child? Only child? In biological families, children have learned how to find their place and how to react; when new stepsiblings enter the picture, many will find their family position changed. As a firstborn or lastborn child tries to figure out how to function as a middle child, confusion about roles might bring about rivalry or misbehavior with siblings.

Although these transitions are confusing, they offer new possibilities. The greatest of these is a new perspective. Children cannot always go out into the world playing the same role they play in their family. A changed birth order provides a "practice session," teaching that lesson early in life. Change is what life is all about! And as stepchildren view and take part in the workings of the family from a new place, they become more adaptable. Old ways of relating and behaving don't work; learning to cope with these realities ultimately creates the ability to adjust to life's changing situations.

As children adapt to stepsiblings, it is important to avoid comparing them with one another. This is particularly true when there are two stepsiblings of the same age and sex. Having grown up in two different families, they may be very different.

Barbara and Ellen are both 12. Barbara likes to experiment with makeup, new hairstyles, and clothes. She talks about boys constantly. Ellen still plays with dolls and younger children. She is most comfortable in jeans, and talk about boyfriends sickens her. By supporting their differences and strengths, parents can help both children feel accepted and reduce conflict between them.

As children struggle with a changed position in the family, take care that no one slips through the cracks. Be sure each child finds a way to be special and significant in the family. Avoid letting the child who took over the first position become the boss or responsible for the other children.

Chart 4B

FAMILY CONSTELLATION CHART

Position	Typical Characteristics	Implications for Parents and Stepparents
First child	• Often takes responsibility for other siblings. • Gets along well with authority figures. • Likely to become high achiever. • Needs to feel right, perfect, superior.	• Avoid pressure to succeed. • Encourage fun of participating, not goal of winning. • Teach that mistakes are for learning. • Help child accept failure and not feel it's a reflection of self-worth.
Only child	• Used to being center of attention. • Unsure of self in many ways. • May feel incompetent compared to parents or others. • Likely to be responsible. • Often refuses to cooperate if fails to get own way.	• Provide learning opportunities with other children. • Encourage visiting friends. • Have spend-the-night company. • Utilize child care and nursery schools.
Second child	• May try to catch up with older child's competence. • May try to be older child's opposite in many ways. • May rebel in order to find own place.	• Encourage child's uniqueness. • Avoid comparisons with oldest. • Allow child to handle own conflicts with oldest.
Middle child	• May feel crowded out, unsure of position. • May be sensitive, bitter or revengeful. • May be good diplomat or mediator.	• Make time for one-on-one activities. • Include in family functions. • Ask for child's opinion.
Youngest child	• Often spoiled by parents, older siblings. • Often kept a baby. • Often self-indulgent. • Often highly creative. • Often clever.	• Do not do for youngest (especially on a regular basis) what child can do alone. • Do not rescue from conflicts (thus making a victim). • Do not refer to as "The Baby." • Encourage self-reliance.

Adapted from Michael H. Popkin, Active Parenting: Parent Handbook *(Atlanta, Ga.: Active Parenting, Inc., 1983), 19. Used by permission.*

If you have a new baby, or plan on one, it might be helpful to know that it is common for children to view this situation with anxiety and confusion. New babies need a lot of attention, and your children already worry about sharing their parent with others. But a new baby can serve as a biological connection to your separate families, bringing you all closer together. Do beware of expecting older kids to baby-sit the new bundle of joy. If preteens or teenagers feel used, everything might backfire.

Special Bonus

Unlikely as it may seem at times, stepsisters and stepbrothers may be one of the greatest gifts parents give their children with remarriage. As they learn to cope with each other's differences and fears, stepsiblings share many benefits. Friendship is one. Many stepkids develop life-long friendships, sharing common interests and problems. As they share abilities, hobbies, and oppor-

Jealousy—even when it seems unreasonable or extreme—is a child's natural expression of the fear of being replaced.

tunities, stepsiblings learn from one another. Friendship, sharing, and learning to get along with others are a special bonus for only children who inherit brothers and sisters through remarriage.

A different or expanded point of view is another bonus. Learning to live with other children, kids might gain a new perspective on themselves, dumping old labels ("Jock," "Dummy," "Goodie-Goodie") that tie them to destructive patterns. Stepsiblings may teach each other new things, providing skills, insights, and a new system of beliefs.

Coming Together—The Stepfamily Meeting

A family meeting is more than everyone finally getting together at dinner: it's a regularly scheduled meeting of all family members. The purpose is to encourage understanding and cooperation. Decisions and plans can be made, complaints and compliments shared, questions and suggestions clarified, and chores agreed upon. The stepfamily meeting is also a time to share good experiences and positive feelings about one another. It provides an excellent opportunity for children to listen and be heard. As it creates harmony, the regular meeting strengthens your stepfamily.

Begin by agreeing upon a time when all family members can come together. Invite everyone, but don't pressure someone who refuses to attend. When you make it clear that the decisions made during the meeting will affect all stepfamily members, the reluctant ones may join in. Organize the meeting with a leader and secretary; rotate these positions from meeting to meeting.

Start the meeting by sharing thanks, appreciation, and successes so that everyone begins to feel warm and positive. When problems are brought up, solve them together with this four-step process:

1. Identify the issue. It's important to clarify exactly what the problem is. Make sure everyone has a chance to be heard.

2. Brainstorm possible solutions. Allow for all suggestions, whether they seem realistic or not. In brainstorming, no idea is ever judged; all are accepted and considered.

3. Evaluate the brainstormed solutions and choose one. Work at this until the stepfamily can agree on one solution.

4. Try out the solution agreed to. Make sure everyone commits to following whatever plan has been made for a specific period of time.

It's important that everyone share in the decision making, adults and children alike. As you make plans for your stepfamily, focus on the positive. Laughing and enjoying one another builds bonds. (*The Encouragement Packet* mentioned earlier in this chapter provides a wealth of activities—some for fun, some for problem solving—that stepfamilies will enjoy.)

Keep meetings short. Depending on whether your meetings include young children or teenagers, they might last anywhere from 15 to 30 minutes.

Stepsiblings can also help one another learn to cope with life. From the ups and downs of stepsibling relationships, kids can learn skills to better help them negotiate, cooperate, and accept. They become more flexible. Children who learn to adapt in stepfamilies may also learn to adapt to other situations faster than children from traditional families. They have had more practice!

Grandparents and Step-grandparents— Expanding Roles

For children, grandparents are a vital connection between their heritage and their future. Contact with grandparents is valuable to children's development. During difficult times, this loving link can make a vast difference in easing children's adjustment. When children's lives are being disrupted by divorce and remarriage, and their world seems topsy-turvy, grandparents can represent continuity. After the remarriage, too, grandparents may provide extra support to the stepfamily.

But, for many grandparents, the divorce of an adult child that cuts ties with their beloved grandchildren can be devastating. Even if they've adjusted to the divorce and maintained contact, many grandparents go into an emotional tailspin upon their son's or daughter's remarriage. It arouses the fear that, although till now they haven't lost touch with their grandchildren, a major move or an adoption by a stepparent might bring about such a loss.

Grandparents worry about another alteration to the family tree: a new graft has been added in the form of stepgrandchildren. Suddenly, the older generation is expected to interact with children with whom they share no emotional history. They have to decide how to treat these new children, how to handle issues from gift-giving to inheritance. As they cope with all these decisions, many grandparents feel confused.

Grandparents who feel confused and wonder where they fit in might treat their grandchildren differently from their stepgrandchildren. Biases often become obvious at holidays or birthdays if grandparents give finer gifts to their biological grandchildren. Some stepchildren may feel hurt by this, and it is unfair. Already, these children have coped with so much sadness and loss that what they need is caring and a sense of belonging to help rebuild their self-esteem. Younger children tend to feel especially upset by unequal treatment. Older children can usually understand that grandparents might feel like doing more for children with whom they share a history; but even teenagers will feel a tinge of resentment about second-class treatment.

This situation is also unfair to the grandparents, who may be expected to feel affection for stepgrandchildren. Grandparents are not intentionally cruel; they simply feel differently about each set of children. Their treatment of them reflects these feelings.

Like many people, grandparents may feel uncomfortable talking about their feelings. In this case, you or your spouse may have to bring up a discussion of how their behavior affects your stepfamily. As always, by exploring feelings, you move closer toward understanding. Once they come to understand the effect their behavior is having, many grandparents will change their approach—especially when they learn that they are not expected to *love* the children, but simply to respect their feelings.

For children, grandparents are a vital connection between their heritage and their future. During difficult times, this loving link can make a vast difference in easing children's adjustment.

Sometimes, though, grandparents' confusion, brought on by loss and pain, may lead them to a more profoundly negative response that can have a destructive effect on the stepfamily. Grandparents may not welcome the new spouse and children at all. Some may not acknowledge the remarriage, or worse, may even try to sabotage it by forcing their daughter or son to make choices.

If this happens to you, you and your spouse must take firm action to keep your children and stepchildren safe from more loyalty conflicts. Until your family stabilizes you may, for the sake of your remarriage, have to distance yourselves, emotionally or geographically, from the grandparents. Although this situation is not ideal for the children, it spares them being caught in the middle. As time passes and the shock of the remarriage diminishes for them, grandparents often find a different view. Then, carefully and gradually, you may all be able to heal old wounds and reestablish the relationship.

Guidelines for Enriching Relationships with Grandparents

• Recognize the importance of grandparents and the emotional well-being this connection provides children.

• Keep communication lines open. Help arrange times when children can be with their grandparents, reassuring the grandparents of continued contact.

• Stay calm. If relationships become heated, don't threaten to cut off visits. Keep children's best interests in mind; do not use children to hurt your parents or those of your spouse.

• Create opportunities for stepgrandparents to get to know their stepgrandchildren. Start with short visits. Keep your expectations realistic and give everyone time to deal with feelings.

• Include grandparents and stepgrandparents in your stepfamily's special activities.

Stepfamily Atmosphere —Easing the Adjustment

One of the ways children measure self-worth is by how people around them respond. From this response they feel loved, unloved, or anything in between. Losing a parent through death or divorce can be a serious blow to a child's self-esteem. The child wonders, "What was wrong with me that my parent left?" An irrational interpretation of the loss, yes—but a common one. As they make many changes, children in single-parent homes may feel different, as though they are not part of a "real" family. During these transitions their self-esteem may slip. Living in a stepfamily brings more confusion; like children in single-parent families, many stepchildren suffer from low self-esteem. Sometimes, while everyone's adjusting, adults may overlook the contributions children make. Indeed, until they come to accept stepchildren, stepparents may criticize, rather than encourage, them. Attacks on their already shaky self-esteem may lead some stepchildren to misbehave and heighten tension among stepsiblings.

You and your new spouse have the chance to make a difference in the lives of your children. Building their confidence and sense of worth requires you to focus on the positive things they do rather than on what you dislike. At first this may be difficult. But as you allow for individual differences and accept your stepchildren, nurturing and encouraging them will feel good. The higher the level of self-esteem that each family member has, the more successful your stepfamily. In Chapter 5 we'll look at specific ways in which you and your spouse can set a comfortable stepfamily atmosphere that will foster individual esteem.

Together, you and your spouse can create a family environment in which children and stepchildren will thrive. As a stepparent, one of your rewards will be a sense of pride from being important in the lives of your partner's children. As a custodial parent, you will know the satisfaction of having helped bring stepfamily members together, thus enriching their lives. With patience and understanding, you both can guide stepchildren to believe in themselves and value all members of their special stepfamily.

Notes

1. United States Census Bureau, Population Division.
2. 1974 Family Education Rights and Privacy Act.

References

Albert, Linda. *Coping with Kids and School.* New York: Dutton, 1984.

Burt, Mala S., and Roger Burt. *What's Special about Our Stepfamily.* New York: Doubleday, 1983.

Craven, Linda. *Stepfamilies: New Patterns of Harmony.* New York: Julian Messner, 1982.

Getzoff, Ann, and Carolyn McClenahan. *Stepkids: A Survival Guide for Teenagers in Stepfamilies.* New York: Walker, 1984.

Juroe, David J., and Bonnie B. Juroe. *Successful Stepparenting.* Old Tappan, N.J.: Revell, 1983.

Kornhaber, Arthur, and Kenneth Woodward. *Grandparents: The Vital Connection.* New York: Anchor/Doubleday, 1981.

LeShan, Eda. *Grandparents: A Special Kind of Love.* New York: Macmillan, 1984.

Ricci, Isolina. *Mom's House, Dad's House: Making Shared Custody Work.* New York: Macmillan, 1980.

Visher, Emily B., and John S. Visher. *How to Win as a Stepfamily.* New York: Dembner Books, 1982.

Questions for Review

1. As children struggle to find their place in the stepfamily, what are some of the feelings they cope with? _____

2. How can you help children learn to trust again? _____

_____

_____

3. What's the major dilemma stepchildren face? How can you best help them? _____

_____

_____

4. What's the biggest problem your children or stepchildren have with their nonresidential parent? Do you play any part in that? What steps can you take to help ease this problem? _____

_____

_____

5. How can you influence schools to be a positive, supportive force in the lives of your children and stepchildren? _____

_____

_____

6. What causes stepsiblings to compete with one another? _____

_____

_____

7. How have you tried to create a feeling of belonging for children in your stepfamily? What works and what doesn't? Why? _____

_____

_____

8. Have you begun regularly scheduled stepfamily meetings? What else can you do to improve communication and family relations? _____

_____

_____

9. Why is the link to grandparents so important? What can you do to help children, grandparents, and stepgrandparents build positive relationships?

_____

_____

_____

Challenge to Conquer

For the past few years everyone in the stepfamily has been routinely spending the holiday at Marc's parents' home. Although Marc's parents think they treat all the children fairly, they continue to buy major gifts for his children and token gifts for his wife Shana's children. They say, "Their own grandparents will give them gifts." Marc's parents aren't intentionally cruel; they simply don't see their stepgrandchildren as they do their grandchildren. This year Shana's children refuse to go to the holiday celebration at Marc's parents' home.

1. How might Marc's parents feel about Shana's children? About their refusal to come visit on the holiday? _____

_____

_____

2. What feelings might Shana's children be experiencing? _____

_____

_____

3. What might Marc and Shana decide to do? What will they say to Marc's parents? _____

_____

_____

4. What can Marc and Shana do to expand their options? How can they help ease the differences and resentment felt by Marc's parents, Shana's children, and by Shana herself? _____

_____

_____

Activity for the Week

The purpose of this activity is to identify those children in your stepfamily who have lost their original family position and help them explore ways to make their place in the new family special. Bring everyone together to discuss children's original family forms and the new stepfamily form they've become part of.

(Younger children may enjoy making pictures of the family groupings. To do this you'll need several sheets of construction paper, a cardboard star pattern to trace, scissors, tape or paste, glitter or stickers for decorating, pencils, and felt-tipped markers. Help each child trace and cut out as many stars as there were children in the child's original family. Then write or have the child write the name of each sibling in that family, including his or her own name, on the stars—one name per star. Allow time for children to decorate their stars.

Next, give each child a sheet of construction paper to represent the child's original family constellation. Ask the child to start at the top of the sheet and paste the star that represents the oldest sibling, next oldest, and so on from oldest to youngest. Share these pictures with the whole stepfamily. Then, together, make one picture using stars representing all the children who make up the new stepfamily. Be sure to include even those siblings who do not live in your stepfamily full-time. As with the other pictures, arrange the stars in order from oldest to youngest.)

Talk about the different family forms, focusing on those children whose place in the family changed when stepsiblings were added. You might use questions like the following:

• Whose position has changed? How do you feel about these changes?

• What is (was) it like to be an oldest child? Middle child? Youngest child? Only child?

• What do you like (dislike) about your position in our stepfamily? Is there another position you'd like better? Why?

• What do you think needs to happen so you'll feel good about your new position?

• Did you feel special in your other position? Why?

• Do you feel special in your new position? How do you feel special, or how would you like to feel special?

During your discussion, be accepting of feelings; don't try to talk children out of them. Feelings aren't good or bad—they just are. Your intent is to understand how each child feels and gain insight into the dynamics of stepsiblings' relationships.

- Kids have the right to a secure family life and continued contact with their nonresidential parent.

- If your children live with you, they need special time alone with you and reassurances that they are loved and not being replaced by your new spouse.

- Children, like adults, need help—and time—to complete their grieving. Becoming part of a stepfamily may mean loss of friends, family, and familiar situations and places. Encourage children to express these losses.

- Confusion and uncertain behavior by your children and stepchildren is *normal* until you get to know one another.

- Stepchildren might have one idea of what they want you to be in their lives; you might have another. It's important to clarify everyone's expectations about your role as stepparent.

- To get to know your stepchildren, plan time alone with each of them and allow relationships to develop slowly.

- If you are the nonresidential parent or share custody, your children might encourage you to shower them with gifts and treats. What they *really* want and need is time with you, not things.

- Schools can help or hinder stepchildren's adjustment. It's up to parents and stepparents to work with schools to gain support and cooperation.

- Stepsiblings are a big plus for kids. An only child may gain sisters and brothers; all of the children learn from one another. Once they move from competition to cooperation, many become special life-long friends.

- Changes in birth-order position can provide new perspectives and flexibility.

- Stepfamily meetings can help improve relationships among stepsiblings, give all stepfamily members an opportunity to understand and enjoy each other, and provide a setting for solving problems together creatively.

- Grandparents are children's vital link between the past and the future. Encourage children's relationships with grandparents and stepgrandparents.

Understanding My Stepfamily

1. What are children feeling? Can you identify some of the feelings of children in your stepfamily? What losses does each child need to mourn?

Child's name	Feeling	Loss	How can I help?
_____	_____	_____	_____
_____	_____	_____	_____
_____	_____	_____	_____
_____	_____	_____	_____

2. What differences are children dealing with? Can you identify some of the differences children in your stepfamily are facing at home? Between homes?

Child's name	Issue	Way done in former/other home	Way done in our home	How can I help?
_____	_____	_____	_____	_____
_____	_____	_____	_____	_____
_____	_____	_____	_____	_____
_____	_____	_____	_____	_____

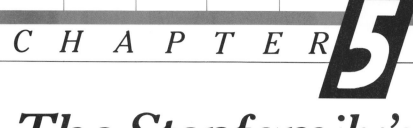

The Stepfamily's Journey

S*ammie stuck out his lower lip and complained, 'But we **always** have chicken on our Sundays at home.' Suddenly I realized our stepfamily had really become a family, with our own traditions and rituals—some so ingrained that most of us were hardly even aware of them. That was a wonderful moment!"*

This book has emphasized two critical facts:

- Making a stepfamily is a process.
- Making a stepfamily takes time.

The first part of Chapter 5 will show you the normal passages through which all stepfamilies travel. With this information, you can better identify where you are now and, as your stepfamily develops, where you are headed. In the second part of the chapter, you will explore ways to set a comfortable stepfamily atmosphere and build a sense of family unity.

Developmental Differences

Every person moves through certain predictable stages in life. Social scientists call these progressions cycles. First, people struggle to meet their own needs in *individual developmental cycles.* Then, if they decide to pair up with a partner, they face the challenges of a *couple's cycle,* surviving relationship stresses in a series of stages—from romance, through differences, to commitment. If they have a family, another cycle begins. Both individuals, and ultimately all their children, are involved in a *family life cycle,* consisting of predictable phases: leaving the family of origin, marrying, having children, coping with kids as they grow, having children leave the nest, becoming grandparents, dealing with old age.[1]

The couple with children is involved in all three cycles simultaneously, juggling roles as individuals, partners, and parents. In any two-parent family, mastery of the phases in the family life cycle is linked directly to the stability of the couple's relationship which, in turn, is based on how comfortable each partner is in his or her own personal life cycle.

In the stepfamily, death or divorce and remarriage have disrupted the normal cycles, creating new complexities. People who remarry may be out of sync with each other in one or more of the developmental cycles. The stage adults have reached in their own development affects their ability to adjust to stepfamily living and to the role of stepparent. Each partner in a new stepfamily may be at a different stage in the cycle of being a parent. One adult may have teenagers, the other, toddlers. As parents, their experiences are quite different. If someone who has never been a parent marries a person with children, the couple faces a different challenge. One may want to have children, the other may not. Mates at opposite ends of the parenting cycle need to give serious thought to the pros and cons of having another child.

Stress can result when partners are in different phases of the parenting cycle.

Although developmental differences can create conflict (especially when momentous changes are taking place as the stepfamily tries to stabilize), change can also produce positive effects. Stepparents can serve as extra role models to stepchildren. As personal growth strengthens their self-esteem, these more stable adults can set examples of success and competence for the children they are helping to rear. Rather than let growth threaten the couple and, ultimately, the stepfamily, it is wiser to accept the change growth brings as one of the rewards of living in a stepfamily.

Stepfamily Life Cycle —Stepping Through the Stages

Keeping in mind the three cycles you are involved in as a stepparent (individual, couple, and family), let's explore the specific developmental stages stepfamilies go through. There are five identifiable stages through which nearly all stepfamilies move:[2]

- Fantasy
- Confusion
- Crazy time
- Stability
- Commitment

In the preceding chapters, you've been introduced to many of the issues that comprise these five stages. You've explored a variety of coping techniques as well. Transitions from one stage to another may not be smooth or steady; indeed, progress is sometimes downright rocky. When you discover you've left some work undone, backtracking may be necessary. Some stages overlap, so it's often hard to tell if you've reached a new plateau. But knowing and understanding the stages can help you gain a vital perspective on where your stepfamily is and where it is headed.

Fantasy—The Grand Illusion

Fantasy is important in our lives. Without dreams of "what could be," we might never be inspired to begin. The problem with fantasy is that it does not provide the firm foundation stepfamilies need to begin to build a life together.

Your remarriage began with romance. You and your partner shared a dream that you could make this family the special one you both had hoped for the first time. By now you may have found that the glow of love has kept you from seeing and meeting the challenges your stepfamily faces. Romance, wonderful as it is, often clouds reality.

We've already looked at some of the common myths about stepfamily life and the unrealistic expectations they create. To further the illusion of a storybook future, you may still be denying differences. Many adults expect remarriage to return them to square one—where they were before their former marriage began to deteriorate. They believe they just need the right mate to succeed. Often, they encourage their stepfamily to masquerade as a traditional nuclear family and fail to accept the fact that the stepfamily, born of loss and built around a complexity of longstanding biological relationships, is a different kind of family.

Another common remarriage fantasy is that a new stepparent can rescue children from the excesses or inadequacies of the absent biological parent—that the stepfamily will make up for the past. Yet, each time the couple approaches the former spouse to deal with child-related issues, the old wounds resurface, and the past intrudes on the present.

Children, too, get caught up in fantasy. Many children dream that their parents will magically get back together one day and restore their original family. As their dream of reuniting Dad and Mom crumbles, some children, hanging on doggedly, turn against the stepparent and act out their anger in obnoxious behavior, hoping to drive that stepparent away.

The perfect stepfamily is an illusion. There are no perfect families. Yet many couples can and do build harmonious family relationships. This kind of success is a challenge that requires lots of hard work. As leftover grief is resolved and the notion of "instant love" begins to be relinquished, stepfamily members move into a second stage: confusion.

The perfect stepfamily—like any perfect family—is an illusion.

Confusion—What Are We Doing in a Stepfamily?

During this stage of development, everyone starts to sense something wrong, but no one knows what it is. Suppressed feelings begin to emerge. Fear of failure makes stepparents anxious; as they try to become part of an existing parent-child unit, many feel left out and perplexed. Unclear roles cause confusion. Reaching out to stepchildren, some stepparents are met with indifference or outright rejection. As the discipline dilemma deepens, tension rises.

Between the stressful tasks of coping with children and managing money shared by two homes, romance can start to lose its glow. The couple's initial harmony may turn to dissonance. Sex may still satisfy, but it may be increasingly less frequent and its intimacy no longer lingers beyond the bedroom door. As adults are confronted with all the courtship tasks they left undone, they begin to wonder about their decisions.

Children sense the growing tension. Their greatest fear is that this family won't work either. To protect themselves from more loss, they either withdraw from, or stop building trust in, their new stepparent. And children's confusion extends beyond the custodial home. Moving between two homes and dealing with loyalty conflicts can create inner turmoil. Further, if children don't understand that it's normal to feel unsettled, the turmoil intensifies.

Boundaries in the stepfamily cause more perplexity. A child may worry, "Where do I really live?" Adults wonder, "Should we invite the former spouse?" Whether financial, legal, or emotional, obligations and decisions that spill across family lines can leave everyone feeling confused. Having to share responsibility for the children, adults may feel they are losing control— a normal feeling.

Clarifying the issues that contribute to this confusion is essential to the step-family's ability to stabilize. Clarification, however, is a gradual process. To begin, take stock of what you have together. What was it that first attracted you to your partner? What promise does your relationship hold? Although this may be an uncomfortable passage, the confusion stage forces you to take specific steps in order to turn your dream into reality.

Stepfamily relationships can be baffling.

During the confusion stage, many conflicting needs and expectations emerge, but most are left unexamined. As family members gradually recognize and begin to understand their differences, they may at first remain quiet about them. Fear of change can keep families mired in old ways because, somehow, what has become familiar—painful as it may be—seems more tolerable than the unknown.

Eventually, though, too much stress and too many uncommunicated feelings will force these issues into the open. When the "leftovers" pile up to the point where they can no longer be contained, people begin to speak and act out, and a new time of chaos and conflict emerges: crazy time.

Crazy Time—The Pain and Disappointment of Crisis

At this stage, highly charged issues find the stepfamily's two groups on different teams. Suddenly everything seems to be out in the open, yet nothing gets resolved. Struggles between the marriage partners combine with those between the two families, snowballing into one big battle. The stepfamily has reached a point of crisis.

In Greek, crisis means *decision* or *turning point.* The final result of crisis is a decision either to stay together or to separate. Crisis forces the family to begin to resolve differences, for if they don't, they see that their stepfamily cannot survive. The process starts with renegotiating, rebuilding, creating a new set of rules for the stepfamily to live by. Roles, communication channels, and decision-making processes are tested. Goals are set. As the stepfamily moves through this difficult time, trust can begin to take root and grow.

Unresolved former relationships, unclarified expectations, lack of information about what's normal for stepfamilies, guilt, denial—these are only a few of the forces that can trigger crisis. Issues that emerge vary from family to family. Two areas that might provoke serious difficulties for many stepfamilies at this time center on adolescence and shifting custody.

Adolescence. In most families, adolescence is viewed as a stage of crisis. The teenager's normal behavior—mood swings, rebellion, brooding, disobedience—can be maddening. As teenagers struggle toward independence, family clashes are common.

For the vulnerable stepfamily, the difficulties of adolescence are intensified because children are struggling to move away from their family just when they need to come close to form stepfamily bonds. Remarriage studies have often overlooked the fact that most children who become stepchildren are at or near this turning point in their lives. When a teenager's individual development is out of sync with the stepfamily's stage of growing together, everyone is affected and crisis often erupts.

Shifting custody. Loyalty conflicts and competition—between children, between adults, between children *and* adults—push many stepfamilies into crisis. To resolve competition, a change in custody might be considered. This

Diversities find the two groups on different teams.

Whatever crisis forces the stepfamily to action, the chaos and struggles that accompany it must be recognized for what they are: normal and inevitable.

is rarely done without pain and guilt. The way a change in custody is handled is as critical as the decision itself. If children feel unwanted, they may conclude they are unloved and therefore unlovable. This in turn can lead to low self-esteem. Custody changes arouse fear and feelings of loss in adults as well. A parent whose teenager decides to live with the ex-spouse may feel rejected and be hounded by guilt. That guilt could damage the couple relationship in the stepfamily.

Shifting custody for sound reasons and in a positive, structured way can be a wise move. But as they confront conflict, children cannot be permitted to move back and forth as they please or to manipulate parents with threats of leaving. Adults, too, must not let intense momentary emotions take control so a custody change is made without rational thought.

Whatever crisis forces the stepfamily to action, the chaos and struggles that accompany it must be recognized for what they are: normal and inevitable. It's up to the couple to help everyone persevere in resolving diverse needs. For too many stepfamilies, crisis means danger. But crisis need not signal the end of your stepfamily. It is really an opportunity to truly begin: resolving crisis is the first step toward building unity and a sense of family. Crisis *does* force confrontation and change. But change and chaos are both part of an overall process—they need not be signs of failure.

During this challenging time, stepfamilies are encouraged to seek help and support. Reading books about stepfamilies, taking a parent-education class, or enrolling in a stepparent support group are all positive steps adults can take. A wealth of fine books is available, and stepfamily groups are forming all over the world. Many are under the umbrella of the Stepfamily Association of America, an organization dedicated to the support and education of stepparents. Should you be interested in learning about this group or forming a chapter in your area, contact:

> Executive Director
> Stepfamily Association of America
> 28 Allegheny Avenue, Suite 1307
> Baltimore, Maryland 21204

If things seem out of control for your stepfamily, seek the help of a specially trained counselor. Such a person can reassure you that you are not a "sick" family. Rather, you need information and guidance.

Crisis need not signal the end of your stepfamily. It is really an opportunity to truly begin.

It is only by taking the plunge—by accepting the risk of using crisis to produce needed changes—that you and your stepfamily will propel yourselves toward stability. You may find that to reach that hard-earned goal, you must first move through pain, disappointment, and discouragement. Most stepfamilies agree that it took a crisis to clarify feelings, roles, and boundaries, and to move family members to regroup and begin to build strong relationships. Surviving the crazy time of crisis strengthens your stepfamily and moves you toward the next stage: stability.

Stability—Coming Together

As the stepfamily begins to stabilize, a key attitude is mutuality, building a sense of "us," or "our family." Responsibility for making the stepfamily work is shared by all its members: every family works as a system and each person's behavior affects the entire group. In your stepfamily, each of you has become aware not only of yourself but of others in your family. All of you now understand that becoming a stepfamily is a process, that your struggles are only a part of that process. As you move to this new plateau, you come closer to success.

But stability does not mean remaining the same. On the contrary, a stable stepfamily is adaptable and open to change.

This stage requires perseverance. Confronting challenge after challenge is difficult, and resistance may be great. Now that you know you don't die from divorce, it's tempting to bail out. Don't! By now, your stepfamily is beginning to stabilize. Conflict can now be used as a chance for learning about yourselves rather than competing. You and your marriage partner are learning to accept one another—even those things you wish you could change. As a stepparent, you are learning to accept your stepchildren for their own unique selves. It is at this stage that your role as stepparent begins to emerge clear and solid. As you move toward acceptance of what can and cannot be, you can concentrate on creative solutions and remain aware of the changes you and your family have agreed upon.

By now you've seen, too, that feelings change. Anger over differences can become an appreciation of the diversity and richness offered by two perspectives. Fear can dissolve into understanding. Guilt can give way to inner freedom and family harmony. Anger can be released, self-respect reclaimed, energy redirected. What was once viewed as loss can be seen as gain. Acceptance and liking can lead to trust. And trust and respect can often, over time, become love.

Take heart in what you and your family have already accomplished. It requires courage to reveal feelings, express differences, and work to resolve them. Having done this, you and your stepfamily will recognize that you've reached a new level: commitment to one another and to continued growth as a stepfamily.

Commitment—Choosing to Connect and Create

This welcome calm allows for insight, a time for reflection. Commitment means choice. It also means taking responsibility for making that choice work. Once you and your family resolve to build a successful stepfamily, you stop playing games that might hinder your progress. Committed stepfamilies are out of the win-lose business; they no longer waste energy trying to place blame for the past. The past happened, and no matter what your family does today, it cannot erase yesterday's hurts.

Commitment will help heal them, however, and so you accept what is and proceed forward. You're able to do that now because you have learned what is normal for your kind of family—you understand how family patterns of growth and change are related, how they influence one another. This understanding came from persevering, from working through earlier difficult passages together.

One man learned that while he and his children preferred to eat dinner late—rather than early, as his wife and her children liked—the early dinner "they" preferred freed up long evenings for everyone to enjoy favorite activities.

A woman learned that when her stepson screamed, "I hate you!" he was really hurting because his mother had again forgotten his birthday.

Commitment means accepting the rhythms of change and the concept of balance—both between you and your marriage partner and among family members. During your times together, there will be distance and closeness, sadness and joy, fear and trust. Denial will be a thing of the past, because you realize that it was from your courage to confront difficulties that your stepfamily finally connected.

Chart 5

STEPPING THROUGH THE STEPFAMILY STAGES

This chart depicts both general guidelines and specific tasks you'll need to complete as you move through the stages of the stepfamily journey. No time period is indicated for any stage because each stepfamily takes the time it needs to work through the tasks.

General Guidelines

- Seek information and outside support from books, lectures, communication and parenting programs, stepparent study group, family counselor.

- Believe and accept that the process of working toward stability and commitment will take time.

- Work slowly toward gaining stepchildren's trust and respect.

- Plan family enrichment activities.

- Hold regularly scheduled family meetings.

- Work continually to enrich your couple relationship.

- Encourage open, nonjudgmental discussion of feelings among all stepfamily members.

- Resolve stepfamily problems together openly and respectfully, looking for creative solutions.

Fantasy

- Complete as many tasks in this stage as possible during courtship.

- Agree about whether to have an "ours" baby.

- Decide where to live.

- Discuss money and discipline issues.

- Plan a marriage ceremony that includes children in a meaningful way.

- Begin to recognize and resolve leftover grief.

- Help children deal with fears and let go of fantasies about their parents reuniting.

- Learn as much realistic and practical information about stepfamily living as possible.

Confusion

- Begin to resolve decisions you failed to negotiate during courtship.

- Let go of notion your stepfamily can make up for the past.

- Say final "good-byes" so new beginnings can happen.

- Avoid taking all stepchildren's misbehavior personally.

- Decide how to relate constructively to ex-spouse.

- Define and begin establishing stepparent's role.

- Work to create a system of shared discipline.

- Learn to share children and accept that they live between two homes.

- Explore any uncomfortable feelings about sexual attractions among family members.

- Clarify relationships with the school.

- Discuss feelings, especially fears.

Stage/Tasks

Crazy Time

- Examine needs and expectations of family members to see which are not being met.

- Restructure and clarify boundaries between the two families.

- Be honest about problems that exist: don't deny them.

- Reduce power struggles and competition.

- Consider custody shifts if they seem in children's best interests.

- Recognize crisis as a need for change. Confront it and stick through it.

- Recognize which issues are not specifically *stepfamily* stresses (abuse, alcoholism, adolescence).

- Identify destructive stepfamily interactions (games).

Stability

- Build a sense of family—"we," "our."

- Become aware of the roles that have finally emerged.

- Connect with family members in a meaningful way.

- Share memories; build traditions and goals.

- Continue to plan family activities and enrich the couple relationship.

Commitment

- Accept that commitment means a choice to succeed.

- Recognize that the stepfamily has begun to feel solid and reliable.

- Be aware of traditions and rituals that have become ingrained.

- Take full responsibility for choices.

- Let go of stepfamily games.

- Accept change as a nonthreatening reality.

- Accept ambivalence: sadness and joy, closeness and distance coexist.

- Restore and renew difficult relationships.

- Begin to reap the rewards your stepfamily has worked for!

Adapted from the research of Elizabeth A. Carter and Monica McGoldrick, The Family Life Cycle: A Framework for Family Therapy *(New York: Gardner Press, 1980), and Patricia Papernow, "A Phenomenological Study of the Developmental Stages of Becoming a Stepparent—A Gestalt and Family Systems Approach" (unpublished dissertation, Boston University, 1980).*

Your stepfamily now begins to feel solid. Relationships no longer require constant vigilance. You will continue to face changes as you resolve differences and make decisions. All healthy families do. These continued changes will send reverberations through the family, causing more changes that ultimately result in still others. But because you've made it through earlier stages, you now know that confrontations need not be threatening. Under the umbrella of acceptance, respect, and trust that your commitment has created, family members can feel secure. You can risk being yourselves and speaking up because you share confidence that neither anger nor conflict will break your connections. In fact, you've learned that facing and resolving conflict actually strengthens your stepfamily.

Creating A Comfortable Stepfamily Atmosphere

As your stepfamily moves through its stages, you want to build an atmosphere that is cooperative, supportive, and flexible—where everyone's needs can be met. In this environment, stepfamily members themselves can establish the rules and routines by which you will all live. When mutual respect prevails, your stepfamily will share a strong sense of unity. Building a sense of family identity and working toward common goals begins with getting to know one another. Where do you begin?

The Four A's

Adults can create a relaxed stepfamily environment by using the processes of encouragement and enrichment. The focus is on giving positive *attention,* demonstrating *acceptance,* expressing *appreciation,* and showing *affection.* We call these techniques the *Four A's.* Learning to use them consistently takes time and effort, but you'll find them fun to use—especially when you see children's eyes light up at receiving them!

Attention. We all like positive attention. Getting attention in the stepfamily isn't always easy because there are more people with whom time must be shared. But children in the stepfamily need attention from parent and stepparent alike. Attention gives a sense of security, importance, and belonging. You can make children feel special and significant by giving them attention in any of the following ways:

- Spend time alone with them.
- Share daily routines and activities so you can talk.
- Get involved in their activities.
- Learn to listen—*really* listen.
- Use schoolwork as a springboard to conversation.
- Find special jobs for children that will earn them recognition and compliments.
- Plan special occasions.
- Focus on a "Kid of the Week," highlighting the life and achievements of one child.

Many of these simple techniques will help you get to know your stepchildren in depth—to understand not only their present concerns but their personal history.

Acceptance. The basis for all successful relationships is acceptance. One of the earliest challenges stepfamily members face is coming to understand and accept each other's differences. You can work toward acceptance by concentrating on the following:

• Treat all family members respectfully, setting a tone for mutual respect among stepfamily members.

• Focus on each child's assets; ignore the liabilities as much as possible.

• Avoid comparing siblings and stepsiblings.

• Avoid playing games like "Who's Right?" regarding differences.

• Encourage children to express feelings and to respond to others' expressions without judgment or scorn.

• Get to know each other well. Ask questions, pursue shared interests, do chores together, inquire about preferences, opinions, and feelings.

• Never try to change a child to fit your image of how you'd like that child to be.

• Don't confuse accepting children with accepting misbehavior. When children misbehave, separate the deed from the doer.

Remember, too, that acceptance doesn't preclude helping a child who wants to change or taking appropriate disciplinary action when a child has misbehaved.

Appreciation. Appreciation is the fine art of focusing on what is right, rather than what is wrong. Letting other family members feel appreciated is especially important in the stepfamily because during the adjustment time, no one is certain what behavior is or is not acceptable. When children hear they are appreciated, they feel good about themselves. Some tips about showing appreciation include:

• Use verbal statements: "Andy, I appreciate your keeping such a tidy room."

• Give appreciative notes: "Dear Martha, Thanks for being so interested in my new work project. It made me feel so good when you wanted to learn more about it. You're a super stepdaughter!" Whether notes are tucked in a lunchbox or under a pillow, children enjoy the surprise of being told they are appreciated.

• Focus on small steps, not just final achievements. If a child has only begun to rake the lawn, tell the child you appreciate the nice job she or he is doing. It will make the job more tolerable, and perhaps motivate the child as well.

Affection. We all want—and need—affection. But even though affection is a way to become closer to your stepchildren, it's important that you proceed slowly. Too much affection too soon may frighten them away. Children may have come from a family where people didn't touch one another frequently. If you start right in with hugs and kisses, such children will be uncomfortable. Your stepchildren may not feel enough warmth for you yet to show physical affection. Even if they do, they may feel the tugs of loyalty; as though sharing affection with you somehow diminishes what they share with their parent.

Appreciation is the fine art of focusing on what is right rather than what is wrong.

What is important in showing affection is the comfort level. Begin with attention and appreciation, and as comfort levels and acceptance grow, more physical affection can be given. Some of the ways you can begin are:

● Start with verbal appreciation. After a while, begin to add a light touch on the shoulder or a squeeze of the hand. Be aware of the child's response and proceed accordingly.

● Use "I like you" statements: "I like the way you help your brother." "I like to hear you laugh like that." Make sure some of your statements are unconditional—not tied to any behavior: "I like living with you." "I'm glad you're my stepchild."

● Be patient about showing affection. Enjoy small successes, waiting for stepchildren to feel more comfortable before you proceed.

Laughing Matters

Throughout the trying times, and during the humdrum ones as well, a sense of humor will help you keep stepfamily living in perspective. Learn to laugh at yourself, and give others the freedom to do so too! Humor is contagious: your own relaxed attitude can lead other family members to look for the funny side as well.

Stepfamily living offers countless opportunities to turn irritation or confusion into laughter. Complicated plans, mistaken meanings, daily struggles to juggle schedules—all present situations that can be perceived with humor, if not sheer hilarity.

Establishing Traditions and Goals

One of the most important ways in which stepfamilies build bonds and form a solid identity is by establishing their own traditions and goals.

Traditions form family history. The celebrations and rituals that are repeated year after year create family continuity and happy memories. Since stepfamily members share no common history, traditions may at first collide. One way to balance this is to create new traditions built around days that have special significance for the stepfamily. A natural is the stepfamily anniversary, the day all of you became a family. Since this is also your wedding anniversary, you might want two celebrations—one private for you and your spouse; the other, possibly the day before or after, a family celebration with the kids. Both are important. Your list of special days could also include the day you moved into your home, took your first trip together, planted the first tree in the yard. It doesn't matter how significant or insignificant the event seems to others as long as it has meaning for your family.

Certain days of the year also lend themselves to traditions. How about celebrations of the first winter snowfall or spring crocus? Talk about how friends celebrate family occasions. Read library books together about traditions around the world.

 A difficult problem for many stepfamilies is deciding where children will spend holidays. No one solution fits all families. Some families alternate—for example, Thanksgiving with Mom this year, Dad the next. The parent who doesn't see the kids can still celebrate Thanksgiving with them on another date. If both parents live in the same town, the families might split the day, having kids spend the morning in one home and the afternoon in the other. Adding an afternoon and evening before or after the actual holiday makes the time with each parent longer and more realistic.

 Holidays *are* emotionally charged, yet they can also be the time to begin a history unique to your stepfamily. Why not create a stepfamily Christmas banner? Hold an annual pre-Halloween party? Hold a flag ceremony in honor of a national holiday? Children love traditions. They will want to share the ones they know, and you will see them eagerly join in to create new ones as well. The traditions and rituals you establish now will give meaning and permanence to your stepfamily. These new traditions will also help you let go of the past and walk more securely into the future.

Goals bring families together. Goals provide a sense of future. With a common set of aims and pursuits in mind, stepfamily members feel as though they are working together. Your main goal will be developing family unity and identity.

To start, have family members share how they see themselves, as individuals and as part of the family, on a time line: What will people be doing next month? Next year? In five years? What does each person hope to accomplish? What hopes do people have for the stepfamily? How does each person see other family members fitting in? What challenges will have to be met individually? As a family?

Look for and define the goals you can work toward together. Then take the next step by setting a plan for achieving them. Identify what needs to be done when. Explore some of the problems that might get in the way. What support will you need?

Family meetings provide a comfortable setting in which your stepfamily can begin to establish traditions and goals. Making a stepfamily scrapbook, discussing holiday rituals, comparing notes about former-family traditions, planning a picnic or trip are just a few activities stepfamilies might use to begin.

When stepfamily members share their dreams for the future, they give each other insight and enjoy one another's successes. When goals and dreams are reached, it's time for a celebration!

Hope—The Beacon of the Future

Samuel Johnson once said, "Remarriage is the triumph of hope over experience." Set against a background of past disappointments, having already overcome great odds, your stepfamily makes its special commitment to family life. As you begin, you believe you've mastered the lessons of experience. Each of you has hopes and dreams about what this different kind of family will be like. You know that hope alone is not enough; yet, without it, no dream can ever be realized. During your stepfamily's difficult early development, faith in its potential needs to be unwavering. Although information and skills are essential, you must also trust in the *process* of becoming a stepfamily.

This process takes a long time; how long depends on the amount of energy you put into it. To work through the stages toward commitment takes most stepfamilies several years. Many get bogged down in the early stages and need help and support to move out of the confusion and crazy time. But once they accomplish this and a family commitment is made, many stepfamily members describe feelings akin to the exhilaration of having scaled a mountain. They conquered the roots and rocks, weathered the storms, and finally stood together at the summit—proud of themselves for having had the character and perseverance to reach their goal.

What's Special about Your Stepfamily?

Your stepfamily is special. Not only is each person in it unique, but there is no other configuration in the world quite like the group you have become.

Reminding yourselves of this often is important. It becomes easy to get caught up with the stresses; you need to concentrate on the strengths that make your stepfamily one of a kind.

As family members work through the challenges, a core of mutual affection and concern will develop. This caring began with your remarriage—your fresh start in a happy, loving relationship. Above all, it is this marriage that provides the foundation for your stepfamily. Together, you and your partner can weather the predictable stepfamily stages. Humor will help you over the hurdles; flexibility will spill over into other areas of your lives. Change will no longer be your family's common enemy.

Your stepfamily is special. Not only is each person in it unique, but there is no other configuration in the world quite like the group you have become.

There's a saying that's stitched on samplers and printed on posters: it says that we can give our children only two things—roots and wings. For stepchildren, roots become tangled and complicated. But, as new relationships take root and intertwine with the old, children's spirits can blossom and thrive. With support and love coming from so many sources, children can branch out in many directions, forming a myriad of connections as diverse as they are strong.

And the wings? At first—for children who have known loss— confusion, guilt, and anger undermine their sense of self and security. But as time heals wounds and trust grows, your caring helps them not only to take wing, but, released from the emotional baggage that weighed them down, to soar. You and your partner will feel a great sense of pride in their growth and achievements.

Both stepparents and stepchildren speak of the warmth and closeness they share. Most admit that, although building trust and commitment wasn't easy, they have reaped tremendous rewards. In time, your concern for one another will grow into commitment. Your journey will be joyous. There will be wonderful memories for you to share. For many people, love will grow as well. And where there is love, most things are possible.

Notes

1. Two excellent books on developmental cycles are *The Couple's Journey*, by Susan M. Campbell (San Luis Obispo, Calif.: Impact, 1980) and *Passages*, by Gail Sheehy (New York: Bantam Books, 1977).

2. Adapted from the research of Elizabeth A. Carter and Monica McGoldrick, *The Family Life Cycle: A Framework for Family Therapy* (New York: Gardner Press, 1980) and Patricia Papernow, "A Phenomenological Study of the Developmental Stages of Becoming a Stepparent—A Gestalt and Family Systems Approach" (unpublished dissertation, Boston University, 1980).

References

Campbell, Susan M. *The Couple's Journey*. San Luis Obispo, Calif.: Impact, 1980.

Carter, Elizabeth A., and Monica McGoldrick. *The Family Life Cycle: A Framework for Family Therapy*. New York: Gardner Press, 1980.

Einstein, Elizabeth. *The Stepfamily: Living, Loving, and Learning*. New York: Macmillan, 1982; Boston: Shambhala, 1985.

Questions for Review

1. Are you and your partner in similar stages of your individual life cycles? As parents? In your professional lives? In your relationships with your own parents? What stresses can you identify that come from being out of sync?

_____

_____

2. What can you gain by understanding the stages of stepfamily development? Can you identify the stage you are in? _____

_____

_____

3. Was the fantasy stage a short or long passage for your stepfamily? Are you through it yet? If so, what things did you do to move on? If not, what do you think needs to be done to propel your family into the next stage? _____

_____

_____

4. Are you presently in the confusion stage? How can you, or how have you been able to, determine boundaries and roles? Expand communication? ____

_____

_____

5. Can you identify the major crises in your stepfamily? Have you confronted them? How? If not, what steps do you need to take? _____

_____

_____

6. What specific things did or can you decide to do to help stabilize your stepfamily? _____

_____

_____

7. What four factors contribute to a comfortable stepfamily atmosphere? How can you emphasize each one in your family? _____

_____

_____

8. Have you established some special traditions that make your stepfamily unique? How did they come about? _____

_____

_____

9. What's special about your stepfamily? _____

_____

_____

Challenge to Conquer

Jan and her 17-year-old stepdaughter, Gina, are involved in a heated argument. For two weeks in a row Gina has not finished her weekly chores and, again, is giving excuses. When her stepmother says she cannot use the car Saturday night, Gina blows up at her. "If it weren't for you, my parents would be back together! They'd understand me—and not make me do so much housework!" Jan holds her ground on the use of the car, so Gina stomps off to her father. He tells his wife she's being too hard on the girl. "Give her another chance," he suggests. "She says she'll do the work on Sunday afternoon." But Jan feels he's taking Gina's side, and she's angry at Gina for involving him. Soon everyone is yelling at everyone else, and things feel out of control. When Gina finally storms out, Jan and her husband are left fighting.

1. What is happening in this stepfamily? How are people handling it? _____

_____

_____

2. What's the result for Gina? For her father? For Jan? _____

_____

_____

3. What might each of the adults do to build better family cooperation and prevent triangles? _____

_____

_____

Activity for the Week

If your stepfamily does not already hold family meetings, begin to do so by holding one this week. Follow the guidelines in Chapter 4. If you'd like, use an activity from the *Encouragement Packet: At-Home Activities for Strengthening Your Stepfamily.* This is a companion publication to *Strengthening Your Stepfamily* created especially to help build stepfamily unity. The *Encouragement Packet* is available from American Guidance Service, Circle Pines, Minnesota 55014-1796.

Before finishing your meeting, be sure to take time to plan future activities that you'll enjoy doing together and that will help all of you get to know each other better. Even people who've lived together for years can get better acquainted!

Points to Ponder

- Making a stepfamily is a process; it takes considerable time.

- Individuals, couples, and families move through separate, predictable cycles of development. The more harmony among these life cycles, the better the chances for stepfamily success.

- The five stages of stepfamily development are fantasy, confusion, crazy time, stability, and commitment.

- Confusion and chaos are normal and *do not* mean your stepfamily is failing.

- Stepfamilies can learn to use crisis to produce the changes that will propel them toward stability.

- Trust and perseverance are essential in working toward stepfamily stability.

- Adults can use the *Four A's*—attention, acceptance, appreciation, and affection—to create a comfortable family atmosphere.

- Establishing traditions and goals builds stepfamily unity.

- Many special joys and rewards result from living in a stepfamily.

Understanding My Stepfamily

"Who's Right?" is a game most stepfamilies play. In this game, one person tries to show that his or her way of doing things is the "right" way and everyone else's is "wrong." Yet in many situations there is no right or wrong way—each is just different.

This activity can help you recognize areas in your family life in which "Who's Right?" is being played. Below are some issues that often lead stepfamilies into this game. Check *yes* or *no*, depending upon whether your stepfamily plays "Who's Right?" over the issue. Then identify other "Who's Right?" issues in your stepfamily.

- Kids do/do not need to be dressed before breakfast.   __ Yes __ No
- The TV is/is not allowed on during meals.   __ Yes __ No
- Elbows are/are not allowed on the table.   __ Yes __ No
- Pancakes are always small/large.   __ Yes __ No
- Christmas presents are opened on Christmas Eve/Christmas Day.   __ Yes __ No
- Ketchup does/does not go with hot dogs.   __ Yes __ No
- Boys and girls have different/the same curfews.   __ Yes __ No

Other Issues

_____

_____

_____

_____

"Pot o' Gold." In the space provided, draw circles to represent golden coins. Then, on each coin, write one happy memory that is special to your stepfamily. Keep adding memories to nourish your spirit as you proceed with your journey.